BIG BOOK OF SIGHT WORDS

Practice Pages with NOUNS

by

Stacy Otillio & Frank Otillio

EMPOWERING CHILDREN
FOR A SUCCESSFUL FUTURE

Copyright © 2020 - Stacy Otillio & Frank Otillio

All rights reserved.

SECTION 1

SIGHT WORDS

132 Word Focus Pages
22 Word Bank Review Pages

ClayMaze.com

SECTION 1 WORD LIST

the	yellow	now	when
big	see	that	fly
down	it	want	her
can	me	say	once
make	have	saw	by
not	run	but	from
and	two	ate	any
help	went	on	just
one	will	please	take
little	eat	do	an
where	did	ran	then
go	you	must	put
find	at	there	stop
is	pretty	with	thank
come	ride	so	open
my	out	what	had
three	he	she	were
we	like	are	after
blue	black	let	round
look	good	get	could
up	be	our	give
a	brown	new	has
for	all	soon	them
said	they	under	of
jump	was	who	live
funny	no	four	every
here	well	as	how
to	yes	white	him
red	too	his	know
in	this	again	walk
away	am	think	old
I	into	over	going
play	came	ask	some

sight word: **the**

Name

Trace the words and then write them on your own in the space below.

the   the   the   the

Color the word.

the

Complete the sentences by filling in the blanks with the word **the**.

We ate all of _____ birthday cake.

A green lizard is sleeping in _____ tree.

Write a sentence using the word **the**.

sight word: big

Name

Trace the words and then write them on your own in the space below.

big　　　big　　　big　　　big

Color the word.

big

Complete the sentences by filling in the blanks with the word **big**.

The funny clown wore _____ shoes.

She drove us home in a _____ car.

Write a sentence using the word **big**.

sight word: **down**

Name

Trace the words and then write them on your own in the space below.

down　　　down　　　down

Color the word.

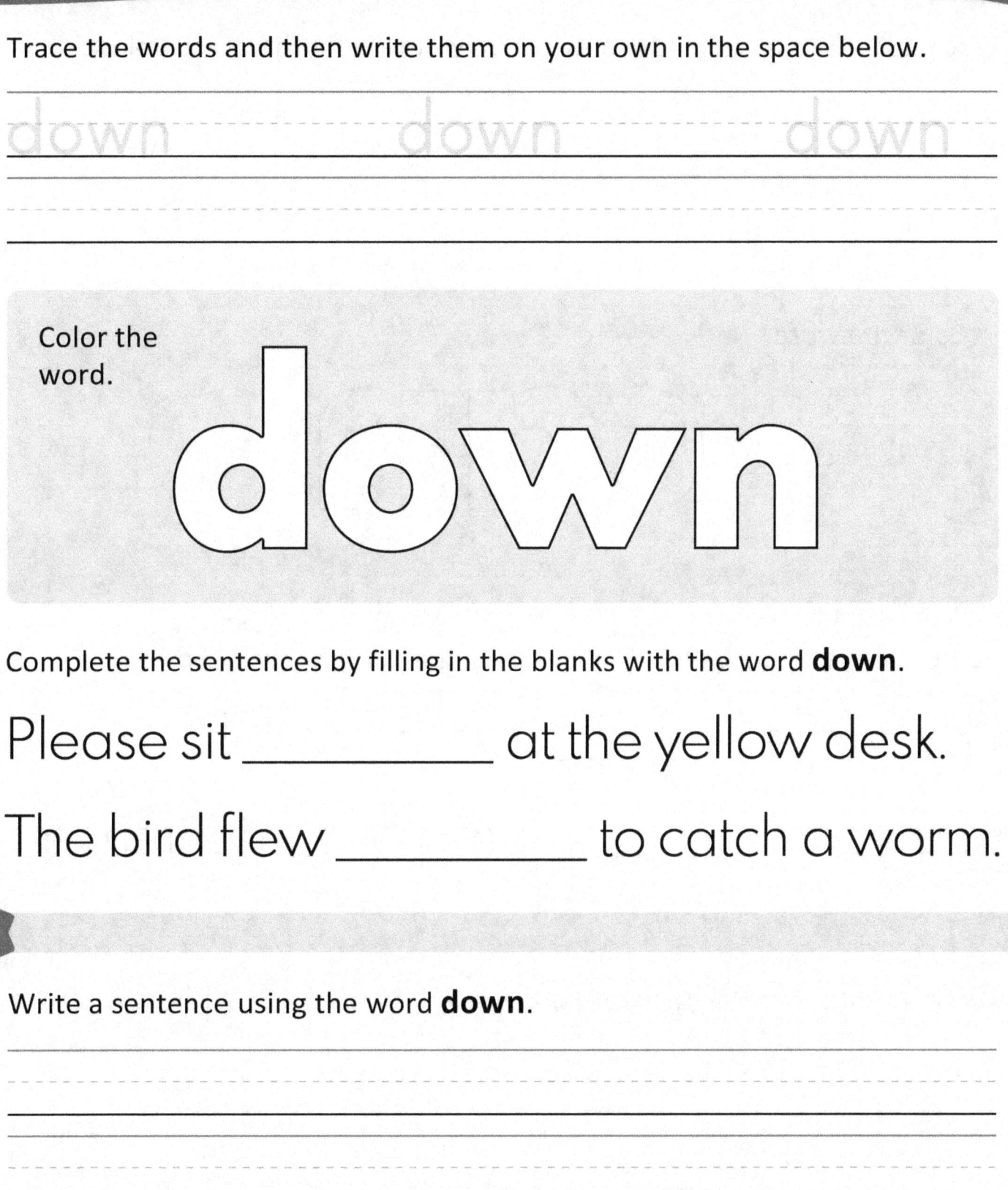

Complete the sentences by filling in the blanks with the word **down**.

Please sit _____ at the yellow desk.

The bird flew _____ to catch a worm.

Write a sentence using the word **down**.

sight word: can

Name

Trace the words and then write them on your own in the space below.

can   can   can   can

Color the word.

can

Complete the sentences by filling in the blanks with the word **can**.

I know we _____ win this race!

The horse _____ jump over that fence.

Write a sentence using the word **can**.

sight word: **make**　　Name

Trace the words and then write them on your own in the space below.

make　　　　make　　　　make

Color the word.

make

Complete the sentences by filling in the blanks with the word **make**.

I know how to _____ a pinwheel.

Can you _____ a paper airplane?

Write a sentence using the word **make**.

sight word: not

Name

Trace the words and then write them on your own in the space below.

not　　　not　　　not　　　not

Color the word.

not

Complete the sentences by filling in the blanks with the word not.

It is _____ going to rain tomorrow.

He did _____ eat any fish for lunch.

Write a sentence using the word not.

sight words review

Name

Use the words in the word bank below to fill in the blanks for the sentences.

| not | the | big |
| down | can | make |

Let's _____ a birthday card for our teacher.

She walked quickly _____ the stairs.

I think you _____ win the art contest.

The _____ rock was too heavy to pick up.

I do _____ want to get my new shoes dirty.

I saw a butterfly land on _____ flower.

sight word: **and**

Name

Trace the words and then write them on your own in the space below.

and   and   and   and

Color the word.

and

Complete the sentences by filling in the blanks with the word and.

Lemons _____ limes are very sour.

It's raining cats _____ dogs outside!

Write a sentence using the word and.

www.claymaze.com

sight word: help

Name

Trace the words and then write them on your own in the space below.

help　　　　　　　help　　　　　　　help

Color the word.

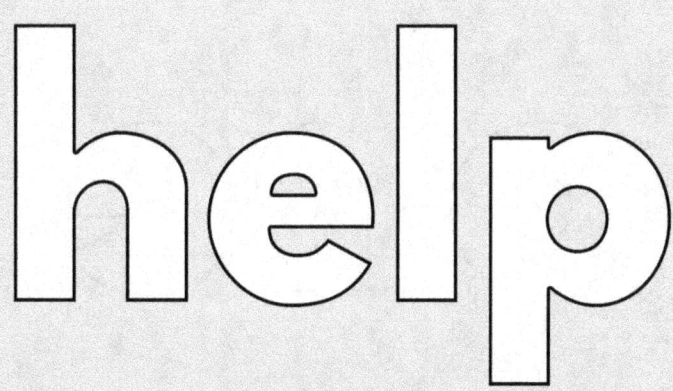

Complete the sentences by filling in the blanks with the word **help**.

I can _____ you carry those books.

Please _____ me find my missing sock.

Write a sentence using the word **help**.

sight word: one

Name

Trace the words and then write them on your own in the space below.

one   one   one   one

Color the word.

one

Complete the sentences by filling in the blanks with the word **one**.

We should stack them _____ at a time.

There is only _____ squirrel in the tree.

Write a sentence using the word **one**.

sight word: little

Name

Trace the words and then write them on your own in the space below.

little   little   little

Color the word.

little

Complete the sentences by filling in the blanks with the word **little**.

The girl wore a _____ green hat.

The _____ duckling swam away.

Write a sentence using the word **little**.

sight word: **where**

Name

Trace the words and then write them on your own in the space below.

where   where   where

Color the word.

where

Complete the sentences by filling in the blanks with the word **where**.

This is _____ I keep my pencils.

I don't know _____ I put my shoes.

Write a sentence using the word **where**.

sight word: go

Name

Trace the words and then write them on your own in the space below.

go　　　　go　　　　go　　　　go

Color the word.

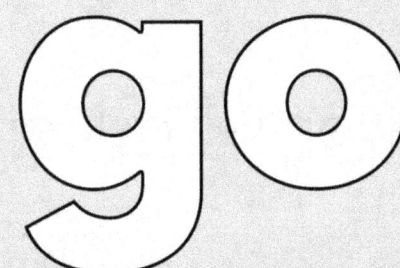

Complete the sentences by filling in the blanks with the word **go**.

Let's _____ to Jenny's house tomorrow.

Can he _____ with us to the game?

Write a sentence using the word **go**.

sight words review

Name

Use the words in the word bank below to fill in the blanks for the sentences.

one	help	where
little	go	and

The _____ kitten fell asleep on my lap.

We ate red beans _____ rice for dinner.

I have two eyes but only _____ nose.

I can _____ you carry your books.

This is _____ we will meet tomorrow.

Do you want to _____ to the park with us?

sight word: **find**

Name

Trace the words and then write them on your own in the space below.

find　　find　　find　　find

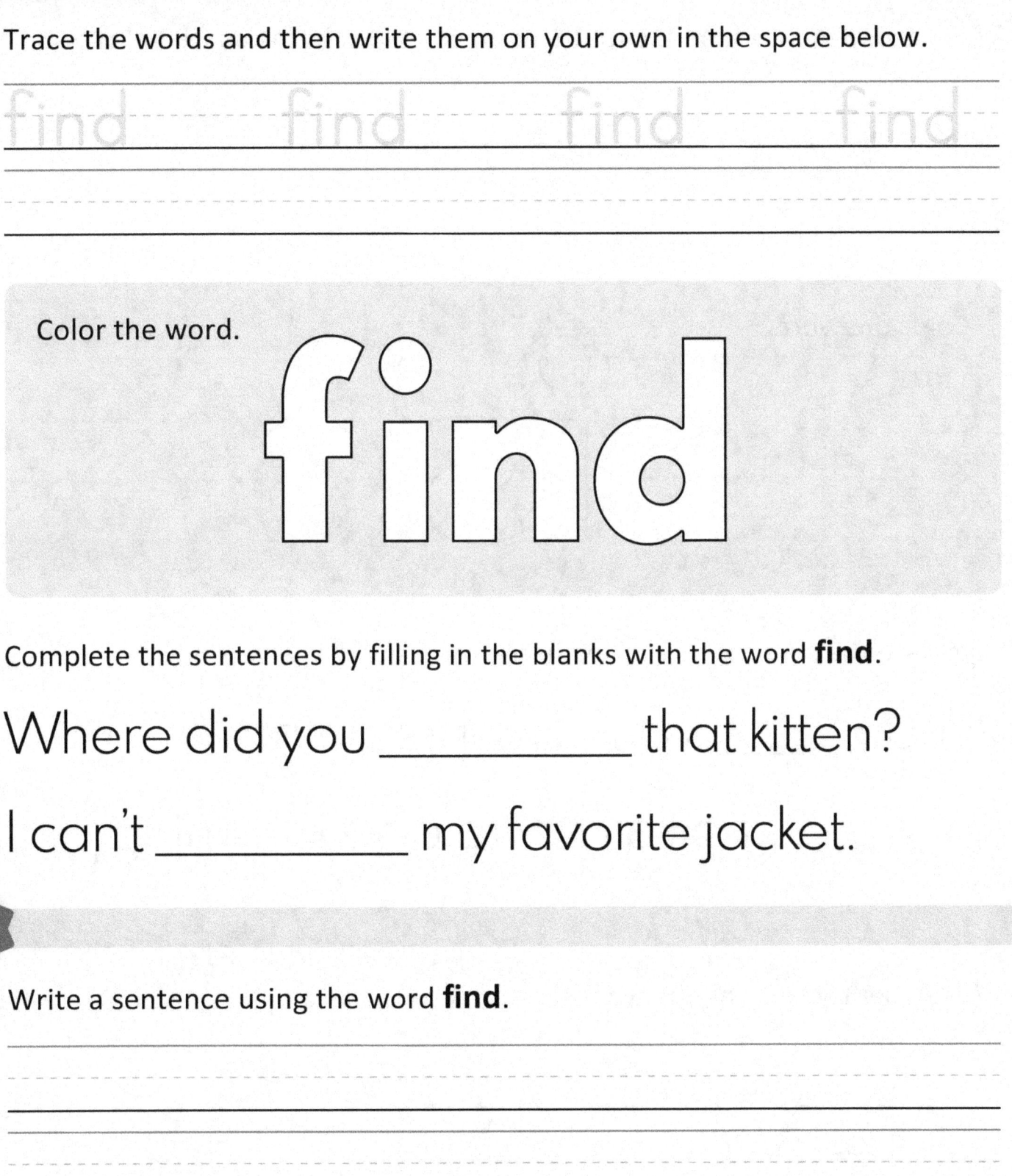

Color the word.

find

Complete the sentences by filling in the blanks with the word **find**.

Where did you _____ that kitten?

I can't _____ my favorite jacket.

Write a sentence using the word **find**.

sight word: is

Name

Trace the words and then write them on your own in the space below.

is   is   is   is

Color the word.

is

Complete the sentences by filling in the blanks with the word **is**.

What _____ your favorite animal?

It _____ a good day to go swimming.

Write a sentence using the word **is**.

sight word: **come**

Name

Trace the words and then write them on your own in the space below.

come   come   come

Color the word.

come

Complete the sentences by filling in the blanks with the word **come**.

I will _____ back later today.

You should _____ to the park with us.

Write a sentence using the word **come**.

sight word: **my**

Name

Trace the words and then write them on your own in the space below.

my   my   my   my

Color the word.

my

Complete the sentences by filling in the blanks with the word my.

I like having a picnic with _____ family.

I blew out all of _____ birthday candles.

Write a sentence using the word my.

20

www.claymaze.com

sight word: **three**

Name

Trace the words and then write them on your own in the space below.

three   three   three

Color the word.

three

Complete the sentences by filling in the blanks with the word **three**.

My little sister is _____ years old.

I see _____ turtles sitting on the rock.

Write a sentence using the word **three**.

sight word: we

Name

Trace the words and then write them on your own in the space below.

we　　　　we　　　　we　　　　we

Color the word.

we

Complete the sentences by filling in the blanks with the word **we**.

Are _____ going on a field trip next week?

When are _____ going to the parade?

Write a sentence using the word **we**.

sight words review

Name

Use the words in the word bank below to fill in the blanks for the sentences.

| three | is | my |
| find | come | we |

Did you _____ the missing puzzle piece?

Jane said _____ can go to school with her.

Can you _____ to soccer practice today?

There _____ an apple in the fruit basket.

She knocked on the door _____ times.

Will you help me find _____ tennis shoes?

sight word: blue

Name

Trace the words and then write them on your own in the space below.

blue blue blue

Color the word.

blue

Complete the sentences by filling in the blanks with the word **blue**.

These _____ flowers match my shirt.

The robin's eggs are _____.

Write a sentence using the word **blue**.

sight word: look

Name

Trace the words and then write them on your own in the space below.

Color the word.

Complete the sentences by filling in the blanks with the word **look**.

I like to _____ at the stars in the sky.

Did you _____ inside of the box?

Write a sentence using the word **look**.

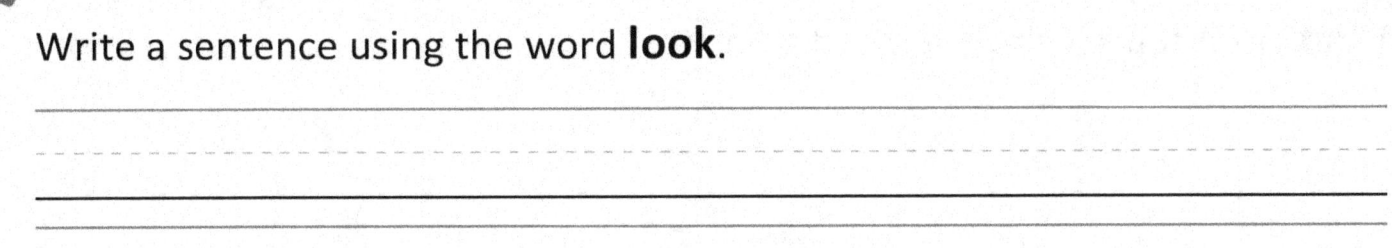

www.claymaze.com

sight word: up

Name

Trace the words and then write them on your own in the space below.

up   up   up   up

Color the word.

up

Complete the sentences by filling in the blanks with the word up.

The bird flew _____ to the top of the tree.

The dog jumped _____ to catch the ball.

Write a sentence using the word up.

sight word: a

Name

Trace the words and then write them on your own in the space below.

a   a   a   a   a

Color the word.

Complete the sentences by filling in the blanks with the word **a**.

I see ___ red bird sitting in its nest.

There is ___ bee flying near the flowers.

Write a sentence using the word **a**.

sight word: for

Name

Trace the words and then write them on your own in the space below.

for			for			for			for

Color the word.

for

Complete the sentences by filling in the blanks with the word **for**.

I have a birthday present _____ you.

What are we waiting _____ ?

Write a sentence using the word **for**.

sight word: said

Name

Trace the words and then write them on your own in the space below.

said   said   said

Color the word.

said

Complete the sentences by filling in the blanks with the word **said**.

Mom _____ we could have dessert.

The teacher _____ to go outside.

Write a sentence using the word **said**.

sight words review

Name

Use the words in the word bank below to fill in the blanks for the sentences.

| look | a | blue |
| said | for | up |

The squirrel climbed _____ the tree.

I baked a birthday cake _____ my sister.

Our neighbor has _____ vegetable garden.

She _____ we would have pizza for dinner.

Let's go _____ at the cute little puppies.

My dad is wearing a white and _____ tie.

sight word: jump

Name

Trace the words and then write them on your own in the space below.

jump   jump   jump

Color the word.

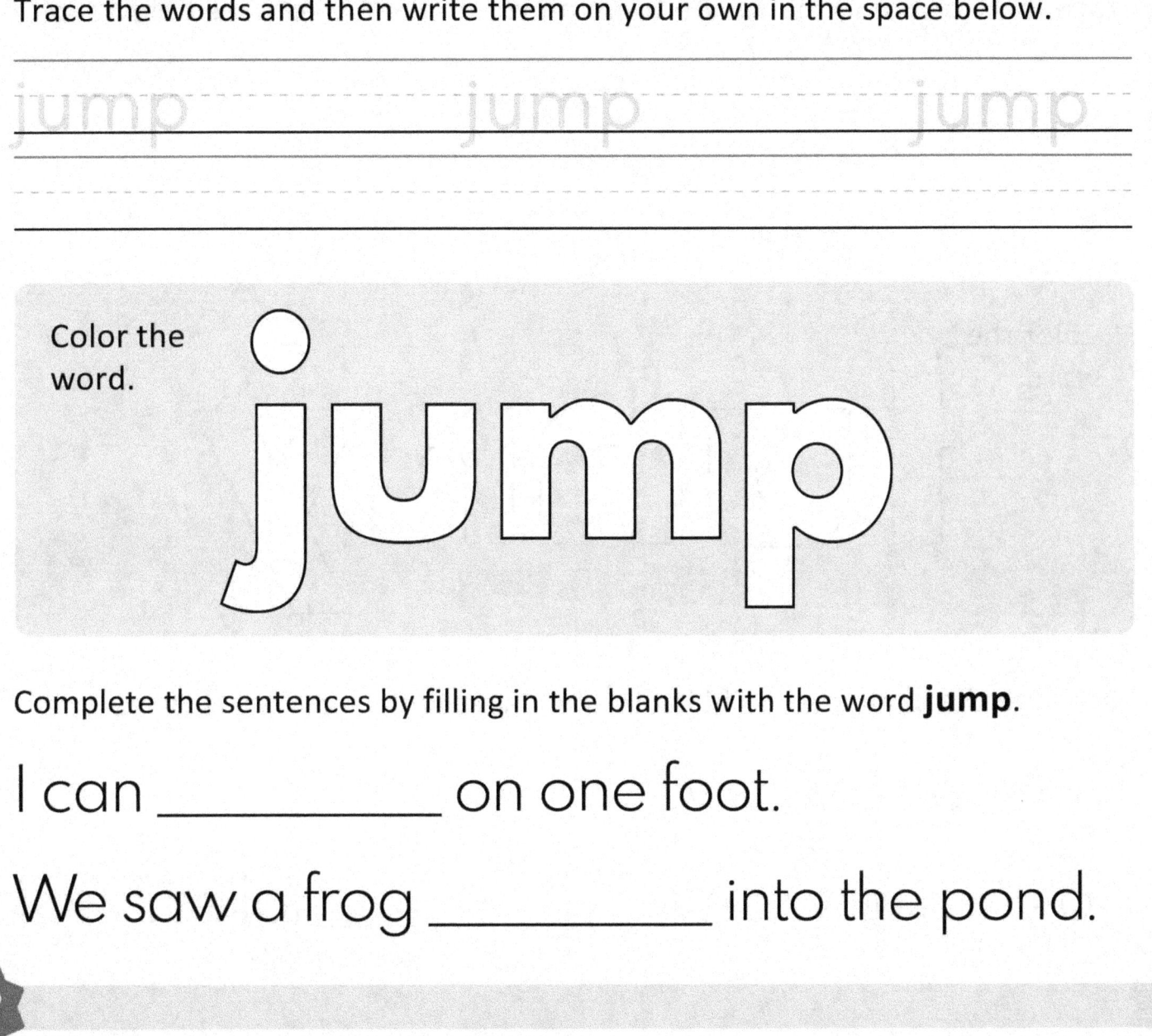

Complete the sentences by filling in the blanks with the word **jump**.

I can _____ on one foot.

We saw a frog _____ into the pond.

Write a sentence using the word **jump**.

sight word: **funny**

Name

Trace the words and then write them on your own in the space below.

funny   funny   funny

Color the word.

funny

Complete the sentences by filling in the blanks with the word **funny**.

The movie was very _____.

Do you know any _____ jokes?

Write a sentence using the word **funny**.

sight word: **here**

Name

Trace the words and then write them on your own in the space below.

here   here   here

Color the word.

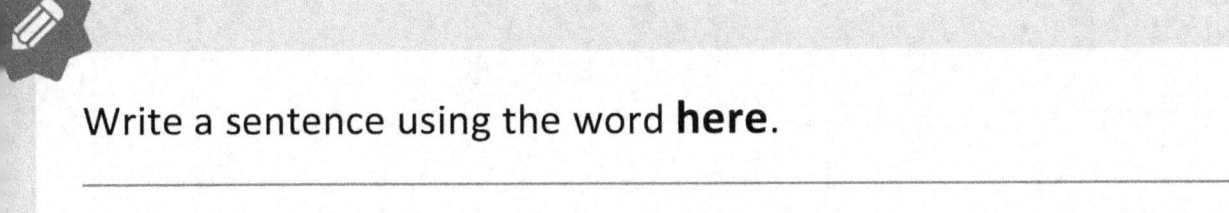

Complete the sentences by filling in the blanks with the word **here**.

We all came _____ to play.

My brother should be _____ soon.

Write a sentence using the word **here**.

sight word: to

Name

Trace the words and then write them on your own in the space below.

to   to   to   to

Color the word.

to

Complete the sentences by filling in the blanks with the word **to**.

We are going _____ Ann's birthday party.

Do you want _____ play hide and seek?

Write a sentence using the word **to**.

sight word: **red**

Name

Trace the words and then write them on your own in the space below.

red   red   red   red

Color the word.

red

Complete the sentences by filling in the blanks with the word **red**.

I just saw a _____ bird fly over the roof.

Those fire trucks are bright _____.

Write a sentence using the word **red**.

sight word: **in**

Name

Trace the words and then write them on your own in the space below.

in   in   in   in

Color the word.

in

Complete the sentences by filling in the blanks with the word **in**.

There are lots of bats _____ that cave.

Look at the baby birds _____ the nest.

Write a sentence using the word **in**.

sight words review

Name

Use the words in the word bank below to fill in the blanks for the sentences.

| funny | red | jump |
| in | here | to |

Please give this lunchbox _____ your sister.

She told me a very _____ joke today.

How high can you _____ ?

Elizabeth wore a pretty _____ ribbon.

Our team will meet _____ tomorrow.

There is a wasp nest _____ that bush!

sight word: away

Name

Trace the words and then write them on your own in the space below.

away away away

Color the word.

away

Complete the sentences by filling in the blanks with the word **away**.

The cat ran _____ from the dog.

It's time to put our toys _____ .

Write a sentence using the word **away**.

sight word: I

Name

Trace the words and then write them on your own in the space below.

I   I   I   I   I

Color the word.

I

Complete the sentences by filling in the blanks with the word **I**.

___ want to play tennis this weekend.

Calvin and ___ went bowling yesterday.

Write a sentence using the word **I**.

sight word: play

Name

Trace the words and then write them on your own in the space below.

play   play   play

Color the word.

play

Complete the sentences by filling in the blanks with the word **play**.

Do you know how to _____ tennis?

We like to _____ tag during recess.

Write a sentence using the word **play**.

sight word: **yellow**

Name

Trace the words and then write them on your own in the space below.

yellow　　　yellow　　　yellow

Color the word.

yellow

Complete the sentences by filling in the blanks with the word **yellow**.

Those bananas are _____.

My brother rides a _____ bike.

Write a sentence using the word **yellow**.

sight word: see

Name

Trace the words and then write them on your own in the space below.

see see see see

Color the word.

see

Complete the sentences by filling in the blanks with the word **see**.

I can _____ better with my glasses on.

Did you _____ any zebras at the zoo?

Write a sentence using the word **see**.

sight word: **it**

Name

Trace the words and then write them on your own in the space below.

it   it   it   it

Color the word.

it

Complete the sentences by filling in the blanks with the word **it**.

I saw _____ fly over your head.

Do you think _____ will rain tomorrow?

Write a sentence using the word **it**.

sight words review

Name

Use the words in the word bank below to fill in the blanks for the sentences.

yellow	it	I
see	away	play

Would you like to _____ bingo with us?

_____ would like to go to the park today.

Our team colors are red and _____.

I tried to feed the fish, but _____ swam away.

Do you _____ the rainbow in the sky?

He put his books _____ when the bell rang.

sight word: me

Name

Trace the words and then write them on your own in the space below.

me   me   me   me

Color the word.

Complete the sentences by filling in the blanks with the word **me**.

Would you like to play with _____ ?

Please give _____ a blue crayon.

Write a sentence using the word **me**.

sight word: have

Name

Trace the words and then write them on your own in the space below.

have　　　　　　　have　　　　　　　have

Color the word.

have

Complete the sentences by filling in the blanks with the word **have**.

I _____ a light blue toothbrush.

Do you _____ any purple glitter?

Write a sentence using the word **have**.

sight word: **run**

Name

Trace the words and then write them on your own in the space below.

run　　　　run　　　　run　　　　run

Color the word.

run

Complete the sentences by filling in the blanks with the word **run**.

Would you like to _____ in the race?

Horses _____ much faster than people.

Write a sentence using the word **run**.

sight word: two

Trace the words and then write them on your own in the space below.

two   two   two   two

Color the word.

two

Complete the sentences by filling in the blanks with the word two.

I have _____ dollars in my pocket.

My sister's party starts at _____ o'clock.

Write a sentence using the word two.

sight word: went

Name

Trace the words and then write them on your own in the space below.

went　　　　　went　　　　　went

Color the word.

went

Complete the sentences by filling in the blanks with the word **went**.

We all _____ to see the new movie.

I _____ to the store with my sister.

Write a sentence using the word **went**.

sight word: will

Name

Trace the words and then write them on your own in the space below.

will　　　　　will　　　　　will

Color the word.

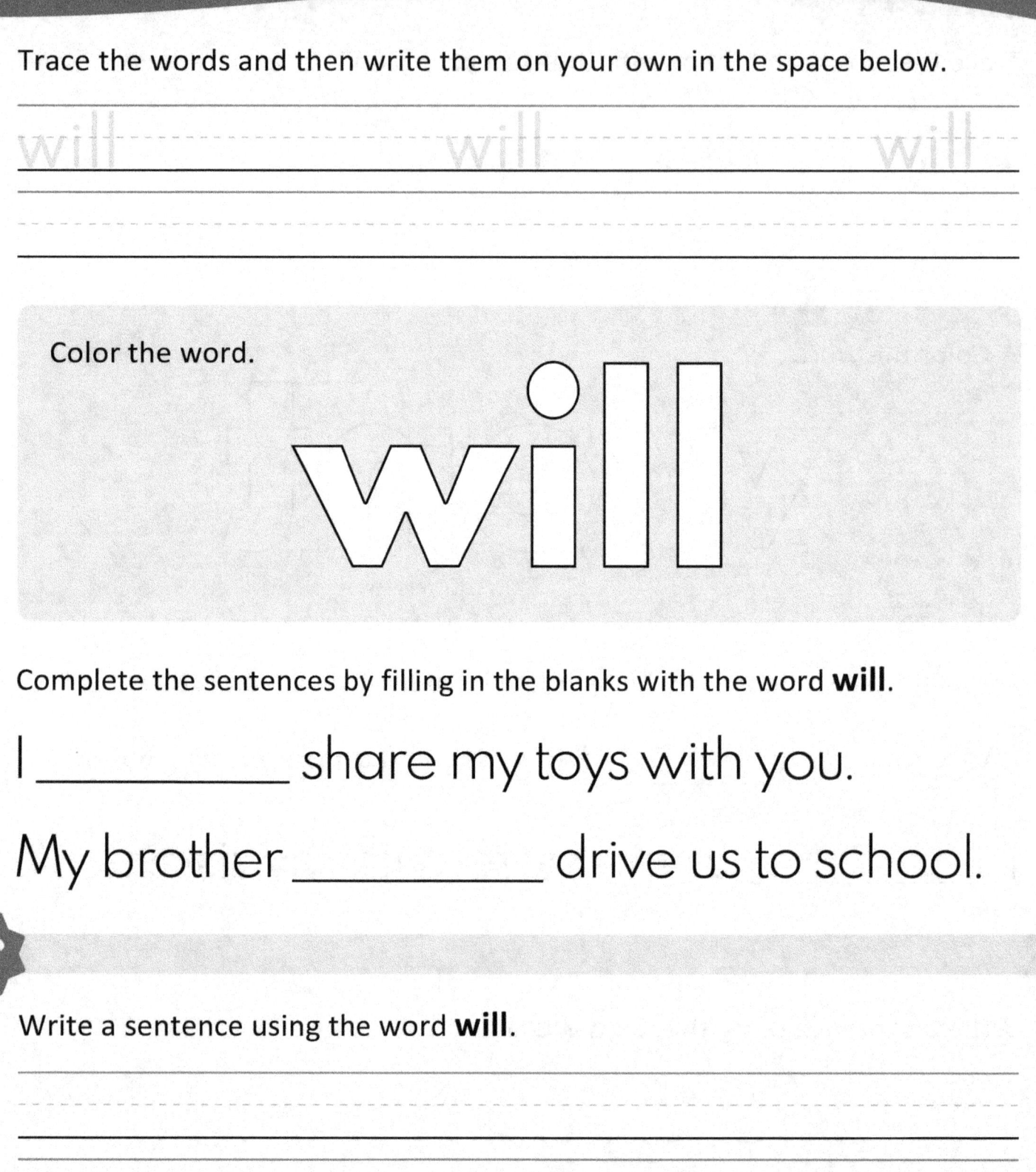

Complete the sentences by filling in the blanks with the word **will**.

I _____ share my toys with you.

My brother _____ drive us to school.

Write a sentence using the word **will**.

sight words review

Name

Use the words in the word bank below to fill in the blanks for the sentences.

went	run	will
two	me	have

I _____ an orange in my lunchbox.

My cousins _____ with us to the game.

Would you like to build a fort with _____?

I drank _____ glasses of water after the race.

Josh said that he _____ carry the books.

She can _____ much faster than Rachel.

sight word: eat

Name

Trace the words and then write them on your own in the space below.

eat   eat   eat   eat

Color the word.

eat

Complete the sentences by filling in the blanks with the word eat.

Let's _____ some birthday cake!

What did you _____ for lunch today?

Write a sentence using the word eat.

sight word: **did**

Name

Trace the words and then write them on your own in the space below.

did   did   did   did

Color the word.

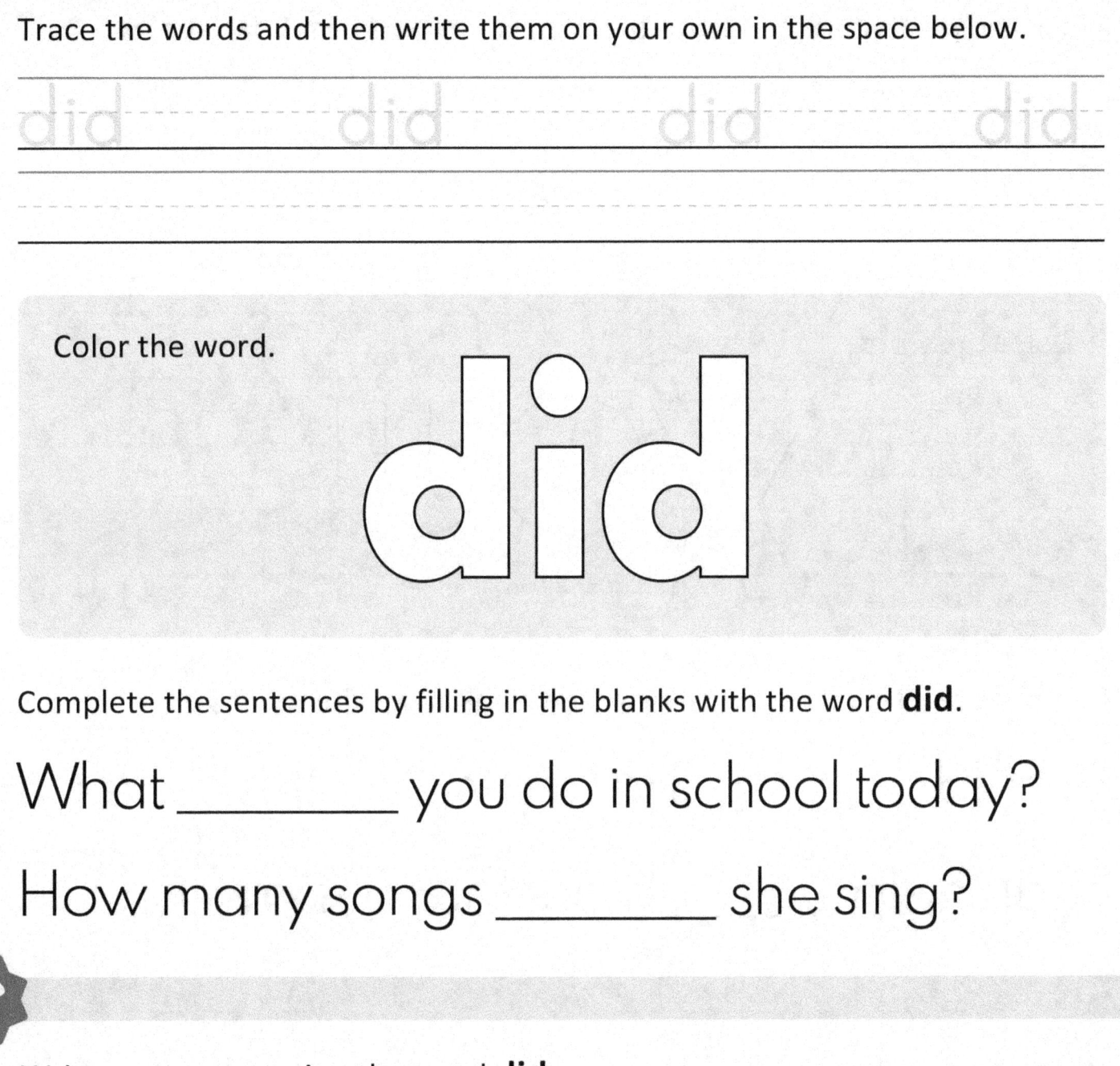

Complete the sentences by filling in the blanks with the word **did**.

What _____ you do in school today?

How many songs _____ she sing?

Write a sentence using the word **did**.

sight word: you

Name

Trace the words and then write them on your own in the space below.

you   you   you   you

Color the word.

you

Complete the sentences by filling in the blanks with the word you.

Would _____ like to play on the slide?

I can help _____ put the toys away.

Write a sentence using the word you.

sight word: at

Name

Trace the words and then write them on your own in the space below.

at   at   at   at

Color the word.

at

Complete the sentences by filling in the blanks with the word **at**.

I saw zebras and monkeys _____ the zoo.

Art class starts _____ two o'clock today.

Write a sentence using the word **at**.

sight word: pretty

Name

Trace the words and then write them on your own in the space below.

pretty   pretty   pretty

Color the word.

pretty

Complete the sentences by filling in the blanks with the word pretty.

The red roses are very _____.

Gwen wore a _____ blue bow.

Write a sentence using the word pretty.

sight word: ride

Name

Trace the words and then write them on your own in the space below.

ride   ride   ride

Color the word.

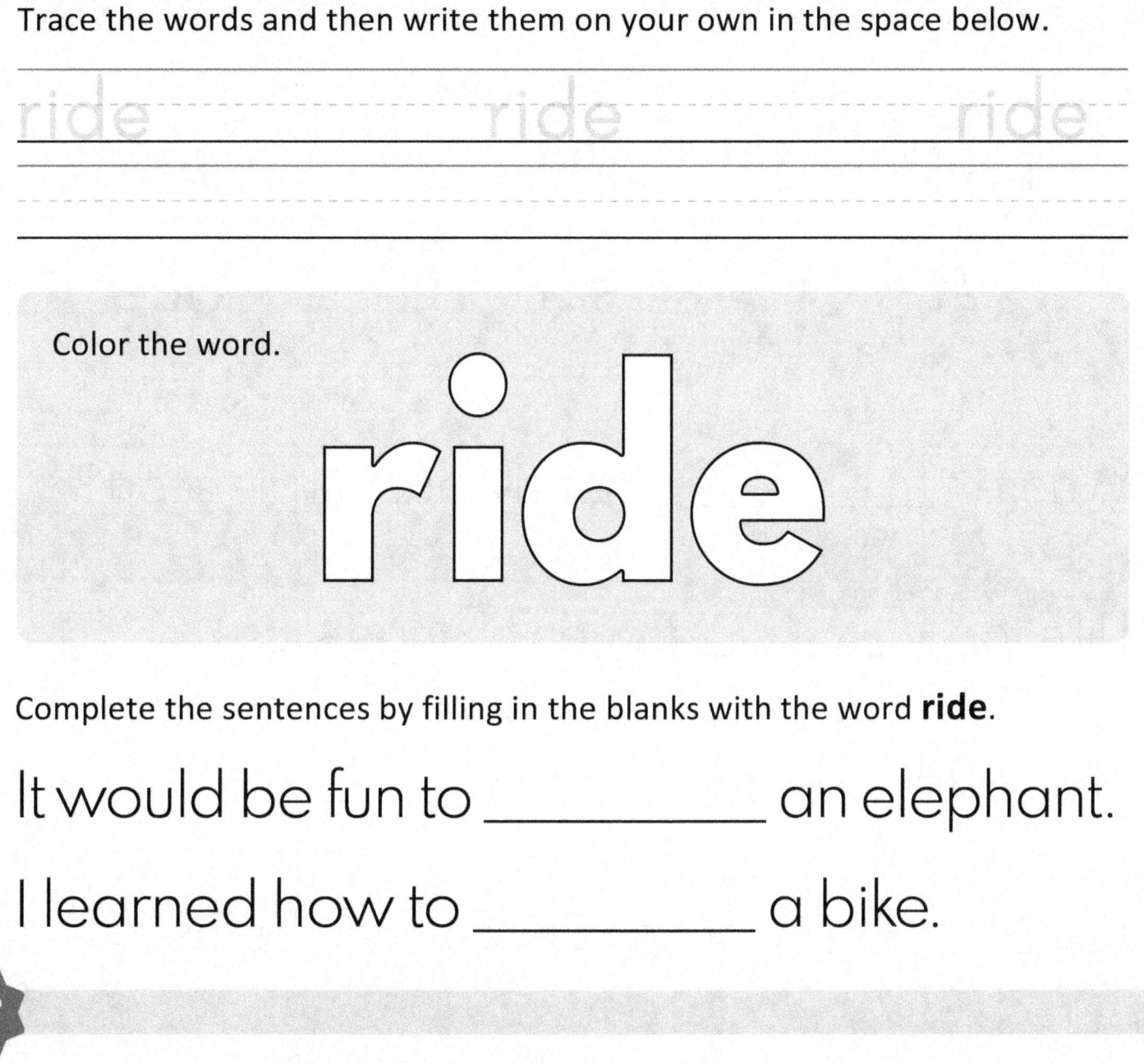

Complete the sentences by filling in the blanks with the word **ride**.

It would be fun to _____ an elephant.

I learned how to _____ a bike.

Write a sentence using the word **ride**.

sight words review

Name

Use the words in the word bank below to fill in the blanks for the sentences.

| pretty | did | you |
| at | eat | ride |

Where _____ you buy that purple scarf?

I like to _____ frozen orange slices.

That butterfly has _____ wings.

Did _____ bring your painting home?

I want to _____ the ferris wheel at the fair.

We saw John _____ his birthday party.

sight word: out

Name

Trace the words and then write them on your own in the space below.

out   out   out   out

Color the word.

out

Complete the sentences by filling in the blanks with the word **out**.

The frog jumped _____ of my hand.

He pulled a prize _____ of the grab bag.

Write a sentence using the word **out**.

sight word: he

Name

Trace the words and then write them on your own in the space below.

he   he   he   he

Color the word.

he

Complete the sentences by filling in the blanks with the word **he**.

Did _____ go to the school fair with you?

Which street does _____ live on?

Write a sentence using the word **he**.

sight word: **like**

Name

Trace the words and then write them on your own in the space below.

like   like   like

Color the word.

like

Complete the sentences by filling in the blanks with the word **like**.

Would you _____ to play frisbee?

What kind of music do you _____ ?

Write a sentence using the word **like**.

sight word: **black**

Name

Trace the words and then write them on your own in the space below.

black   black   black

Color the word.

black

Complete the sentences by filling in the blanks with the word black.

That red ladybug has _____ spots.

The puppy's _____ fur is very soft.

Write a sentence using the word black.

sight word: good

Name

Trace the words and then write them on your own in the space below.

Color the word.

Complete the sentences by filling in the blanks with the word **good**.

Fred is reading a _____ book.

Kim is always in a _____ mood.

Write a sentence using the word **good**.

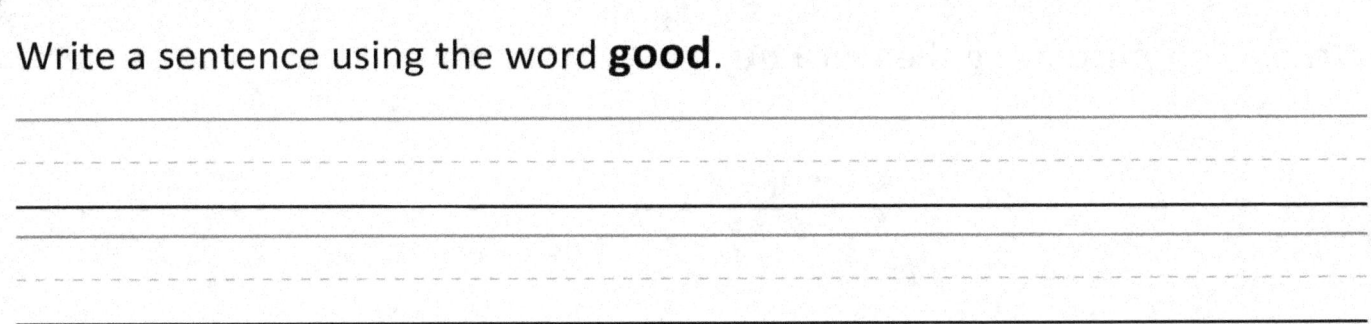

sight word: be

Name

Trace the words and then write them on your own in the space below.

be   be   be   be

Color the word.

be

Complete the sentences by filling in the blanks with the word **be**.

He will _____ home at three o'clock.

We must not _____ late for the party.

Write a sentence using the word **be**.

sight words review

Name

Use the words in the word bank below to fill in the blanks for the sentences.

| be | like | black |
| good | out | he |

Does _____ know how to ride a bicycle?

She took some coins _____ of her pocket.

The feathers on the crow are _____.

I _____ to go swimming in the summer.

Dogs have a very _____ sense of smell.

Are you going to _____ in the play?

sight word: **brown**

Name

Trace the words and then write them on your own in the space below.

brown   brown   brown

Color the word.

brown

Complete the sentences by filling in the blanks with the word **brown**.

The _____ bear ate some berries.

She colored the little horse _____.

Write a sentence using the word **brown**.

sight word: all

Name

Trace the words and then write them on your own in the space below.

all   all   all   all

Color the word.

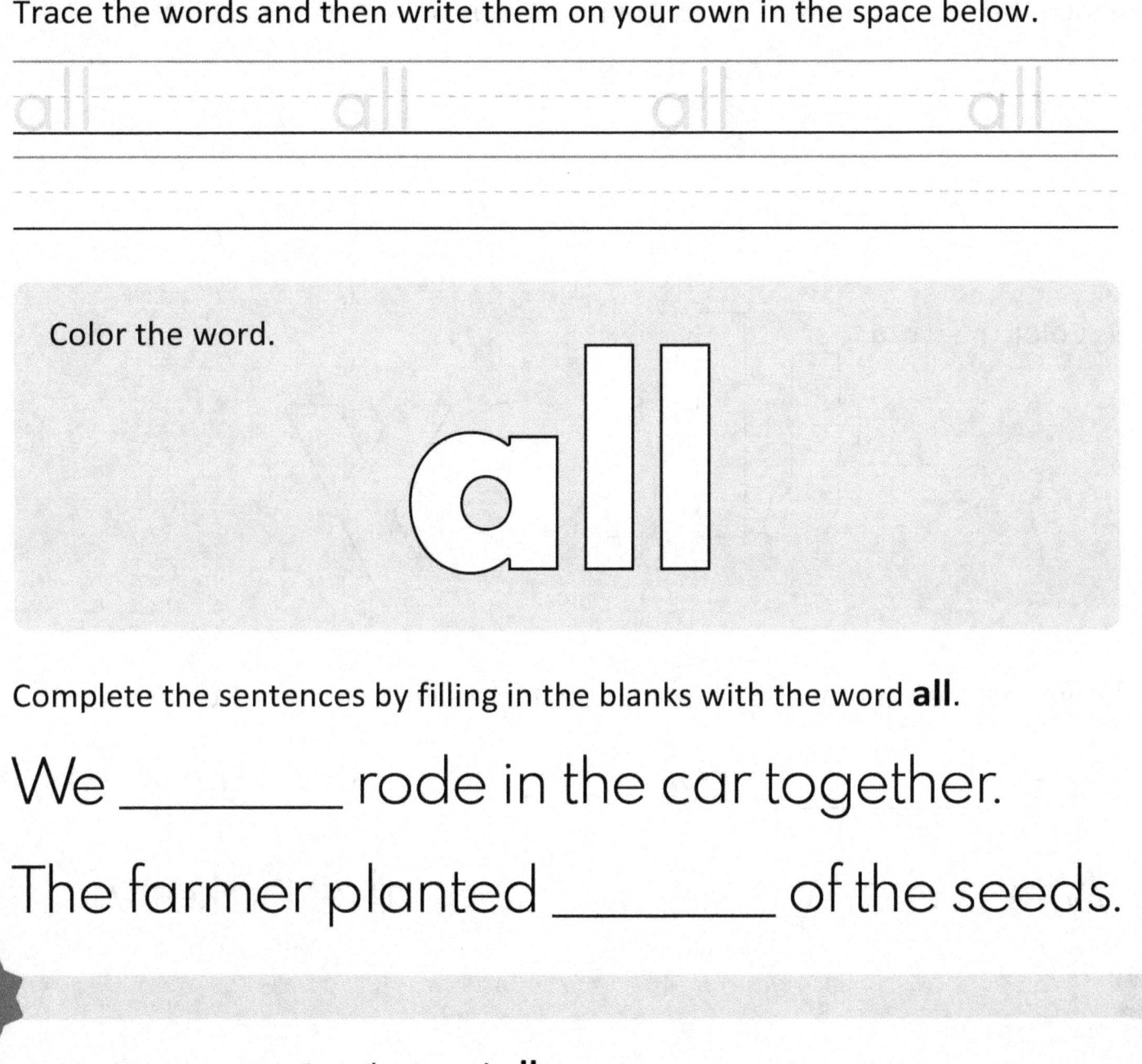

Complete the sentences by filling in the blanks with the word **all**.

We _____ rode in the car together.

The farmer planted _____ of the seeds.

Write a sentence using the word **all**.

sight word: they

Name

Trace the words and then write them on your own in the space below.

they   they   they

Color the word.

they

Complete the sentences by filling in the blanks with the word **they**.

Did _____ watch the movie last night?

When did _____ go to the bakery?

Write a sentence using the word **they**.

sight word: **was**

Name

Trace the words and then write them on your own in the space below.

was   was   was   was

Color the word.

was

Complete the sentences by filling in the blanks with the word **was**.

The little kitten _____ playing with yarn.

Tiffany _____ in my kindergarten class.

Write a sentence using the word **was**.

sight word: no

Name

Trace the words and then write them on your own in the space below.

no　　　　no　　　　no　　　　no

Color the word.

no

Complete the sentences by filling in the blanks with the word **no**.

We have _____ school next week.

There is _____ more ice cream left.

Write a sentence using the word **no**.

sight word: well

Trace the words and then write them on your own in the space below.

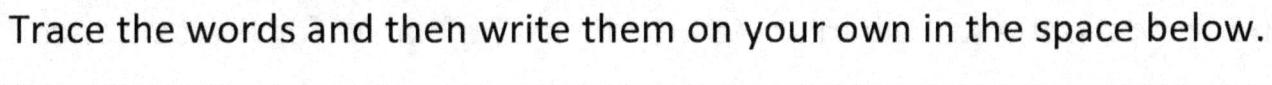

Color the word.

Complete the sentences by filling in the blanks with the word **well**.

Are you feeling _____ today?

Jason plays the guitar _____.

Write a sentence using the word **well**.

sight words review

Name

Use the words in the word bank below to fill in the blanks for the sentences.

all	no	they
brown	well	was

He ate _____ of his lunch before he left.

Did you sleep _____ last night?

She _____ feeding geese at the pond.

The little fox's eyes were light _____.

There are _____ clouds in the sky today.

I think _____ will be here tomorrow.

sight word: yes

Trace the words and then write them on your own in the space below.

yes　　　yes　　　yes　　　yes

Color the word.

Complete the sentences by filling in the blanks with the word **yes**.

Did David say _____ or no?

The answer to the question is _____.

Write a sentence using the word **yes**.

sight word: **too**

Name

Trace the words and then write them on your own in the space below.

too   too   too   too

Color the word.

too

Complete the sentences by filling in the blanks with the word **too**.

The water is _____ cold for swimming.

This food is _____ spicy!

Write a sentence using the word **too**.

sight word: **this**

Name

Trace the words and then write them on your own in the space below.

this   this   this

Color the word.

this

Complete the sentences by filling in the blanks with the word **this**.

Please give _____ blanket to Amy.

Where did you find _____ pretty rock?

Write a sentence using the word **this**.

sight word: **am**

Name

Trace the words and then write them on your own in the space below.

am   am   am   am

Color the word.

am

Complete the sentences by filling in the blanks with the word **am**.

I _____ two inches taller than she is.

I will let you know when I _____ ready.

Write a sentence using the word **am**.

sight word: into

Name

Trace the words and then write them on your own in the space below.

into　　　　　　　　into　　　　　　　　into

Color the word.

into

Complete the sentences by filling in the blanks with the word **into**.

Throw the ball _____ the basket.

They walked far _____ the woods.

Write a sentence using the word **into**.

sight word: came

Name

Trace the words and then write them on your own in the space below.

came   came   came

Color the word.

came

Complete the sentences by filling in the blanks with the word **came**.

They _____ to visit us on Friday.

My sister _____ to school with me.

Write a sentence using the word **came**.

sight words review

Name

Use the words in the word bank below to fill in the blanks for the sentences.

| came | into | this |
| am | too | yes |

Is that box _____ heavy to pick up?

My brother is one year older than I _____.

My friends _____ over to my house today.

She went _____ her room to play.

Do you think he will say _____ or no?

Is _____ the toy you want to borrow?

sight word: now

Name

Trace the words and then write them on your own in the space below.

now   now   now   now

Color the word.

now

Complete the sentences by filling in the blanks with the word **now**.

It is raining. We should leave _____.

I think it's Marvin's turn _____.

Write a sentence using the word **now**.

_____
_____
_____

sight word: **that**

Name

Trace the words and then write them on your own in the space below.

that   *that*   *that*

Color the word.

that

Complete the sentences by filling in the blanks with the word **that**.

We should play _____ game outside.

Don't press _____ big red button!

Write a sentence using the word **that**.

sight word: want

Name

Trace the words and then write them on your own in the space below.

want   want   want

Color the word.

want

Complete the sentences by filling in the blanks with the word **want**.

Do you _____ to go skating with us?

I _____ to feed the little calf.

Write a sentence using the word **want**.

sight word: say

Name

Trace the words and then write them on your own in the space below.

say	say	say	say

Color the word.

say

Complete the sentences by filling in the blanks with the word **say**.

What did she _____ on the phone?

Did Mike _____ where he was going?

Write a sentence using the word **say**.

sight word: saw

Name

Trace the words and then write them on your own in the space below.

saw   saw   saw   saw

Color the word.

saw

Complete the sentences by filling in the blanks with the word saw.

We _____ lots of stars in the sky.

He _____ a baby alligator by the river.

Write a sentence using the word saw.

sight word: **but**

Name

Trace the words and then write them on your own in the space below.

but   but   but   but

Color the word.

but

Complete the sentences by filling in the blanks with the word **but**.

I know how to dance, _____ I can't sing.

I like to draw, _____ painting is more fun.

Write a sentence using the word **but**.

sight words review

Name

Use the words in the word bank below to fill in the sentences.

| want | now | say |
| saw | but | that |

May I use _____ glass for my juice?

We _____ some jellyfish in the water.

I think it's time to go home _____.

I like grapes, _____ I don't like raisins.

Did she _____ how much it will cost?

Do you _____ to go bowling with us?

sight word: ate

Name

Trace the words and then write them on your own in the space below.

ate   ate   ate   ate

Color the word.

ate

Complete the sentences by filling in the blanks with the word **ate**.

John _____ some ice cream after lunch.

We _____ cereal for breakfast today.

Write a sentence using the word **ate**.

sight word: on

Name

Trace the words and then write them on your own in the space below.

on on on on

Color the word.

on

Complete the sentences by filling in the blanks with the word **on**.

Dan will turn _____ the ceiling fan.

He left his favorite toy _____ the desk.

Write a sentence using the word **on**.

sight word: **please**

Name

Trace the words and then write them on your own in the space below.

please   please   please

Color the word.

please

Complete the sentences by filling in the blanks with the word **please**.

Will you _____ take a picture of us?

May I have some soup, _____ ?

Write a sentence using the word **please**.

sight word: do

Name

Trace the words and then write them on your own in the space below.

do   do   do   do

Color the word.

do

Complete the sentences by filling in the blanks with the word **do**.

When _____ you want us to visit?

Which sports _____ you like to play?

Write a sentence using the word **do**.

sight word: ran

Name

Trace the words and then write them on your own in the space below.

ran   ran   ran   ran

Color the word.

ran

Complete the sentences by filling in the blanks with the word **ran**.

The mouse _____ away from the cat.

We all _____ onto the soccer field.

Write a sentence using the word **ran**.

sight word: must

Name

Trace the words and then write them on your own in the space below.

must   must   must

Color the word.

must

Complete the sentences by filling in the blanks with the word **must**.

We _____ eat our breakfast first.

Oops! I _____ have made a mistake.

Write a sentence using the word **must**.

sight words review

Name

Use the words in the word bank below to fill in the blanks for the sentences.

| please | ran | on |
| do | ate | must |

I _____ a peanut butter and jelly sandwich.

Let's _____ something different today.

The two dogs _____ across our front lawn.

He put his new toys _____ the bottom shelf.

Will you _____ help me with my homework?

We _____ hurry or we will be late.

sight word: **there**

Name

Trace the words and then write them on your own in the space below.

there   there   there

Color the word.

there

Complete the sentences by filling in the blanks with the word **there**.

Are _____ any squirrels in the tree?

Brenda is standing over _____ .

Write a sentence using the word **there**.

sight word: with

Trace the words and then write them on your own in the space below.

with　　　　　　　　with　　　　　　　　with

Color the word.

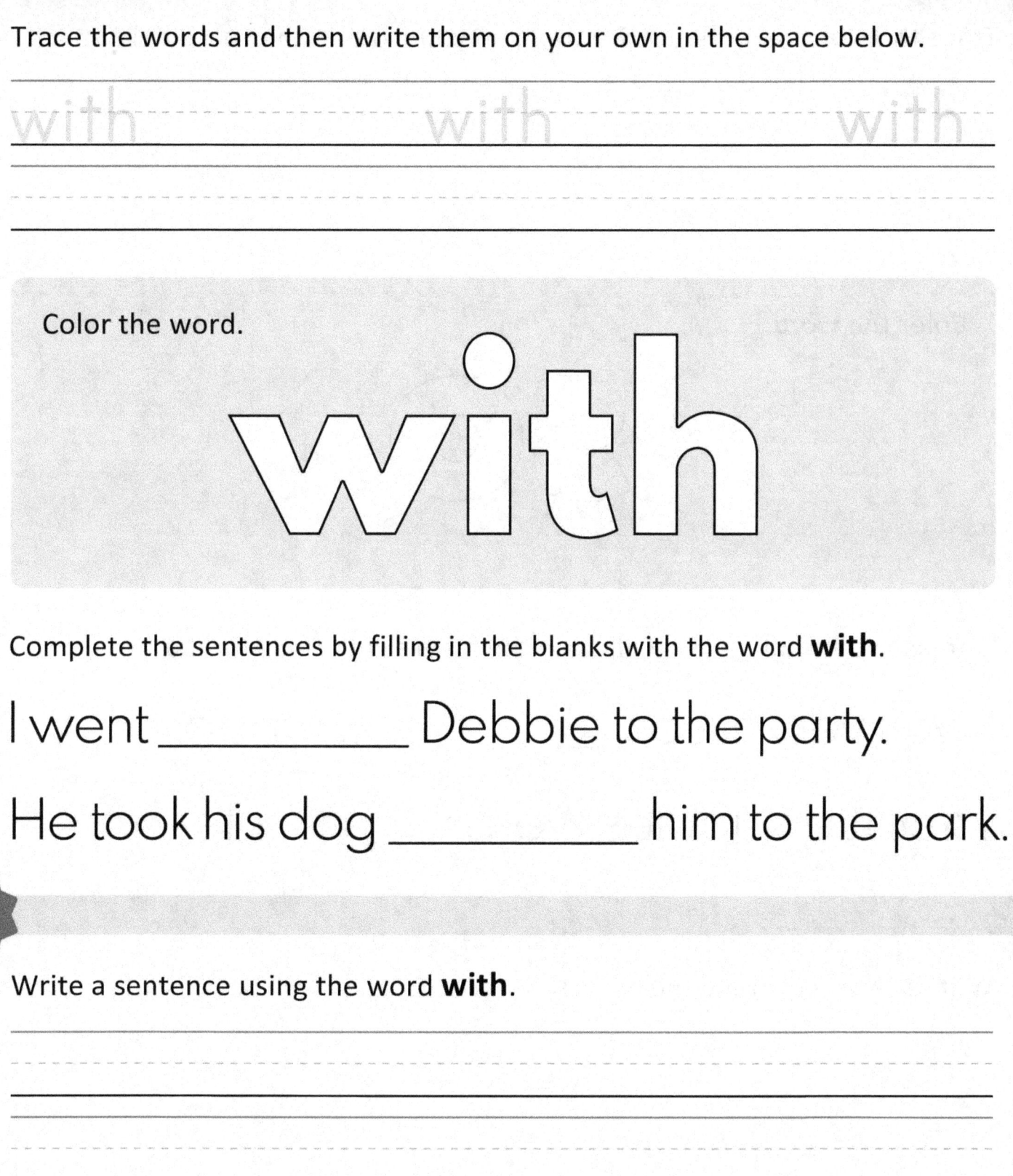

Complete the sentences by filling in the blanks with the word **with**.

I went _____ Debbie to the party.

He took his dog _____ him to the park.

Write a sentence using the word **with**.

sight word: so

Name

Trace the words and then write them on your own in the space below.

so   so   so   so

Color the word.

so

Complete the sentences by filling in the blanks with the word **so**.

I was very tired, _____ I took a nap.

The little puppies were _____ cute!

Write a sentence using the word **so**.

sight word: what

Name

Trace the words and then write them on your own in the space below.

what   what   what

Color the word.

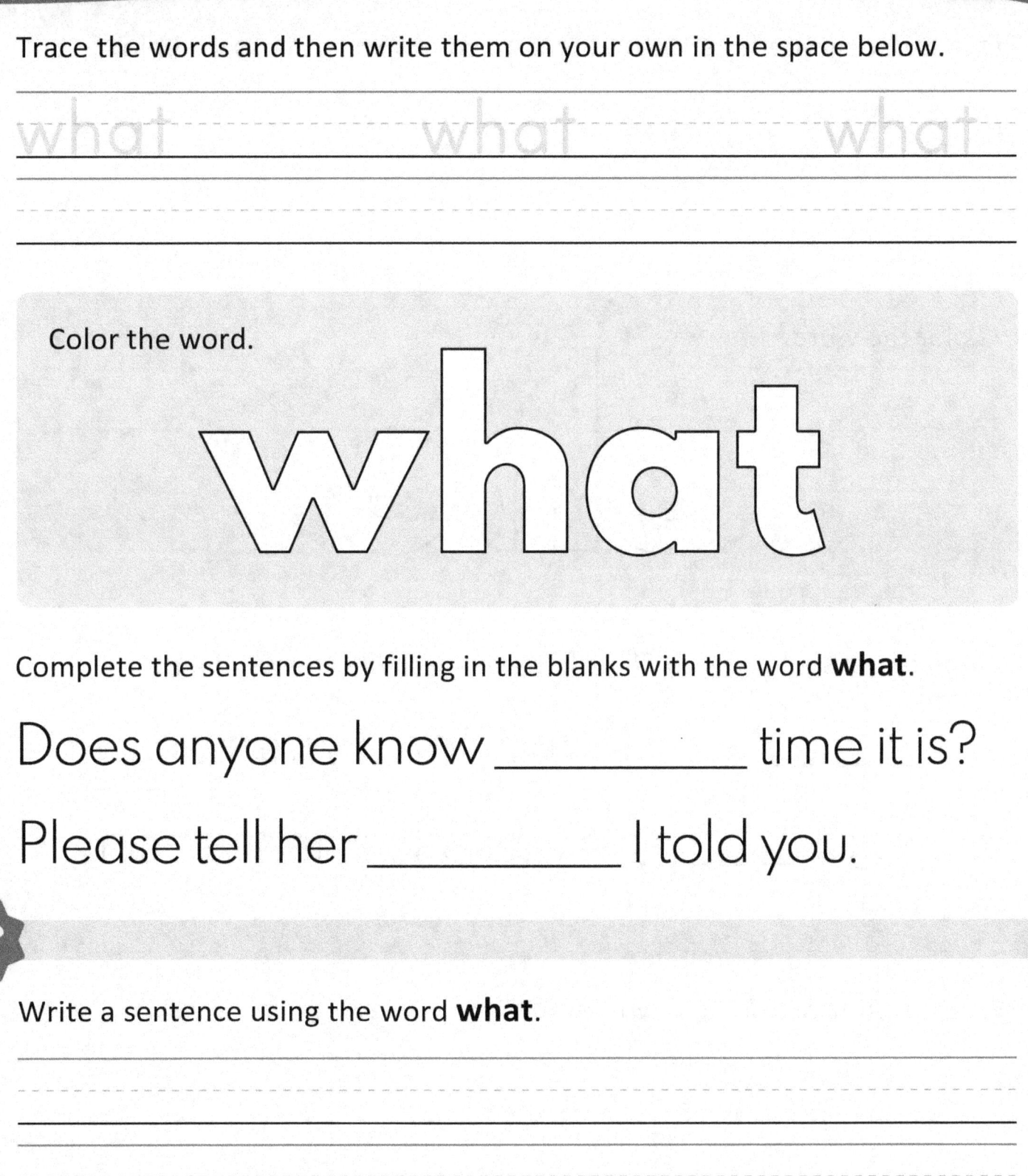

Complete the sentences by filling in the blanks with the word **what**.

Does anyone know _____ time it is?

Please tell her _____ I told you.

Write a sentence using the word **what**.

sight word: she

Name

Trace the words and then write them on your own in the space below.

she   she   she   she

Color the word.

she

Complete the sentences by filling in the blanks with the word **she**.

Did _____ go to the library yesterday?

Jan said _____ would be here soon.

Write a sentence using the word **she**.

sight word: **are**

Name

Trace the words and then write them on your own in the space below.

are   are   are   are

Color the word.

are

Complete the sentences by filling in the blanks with the word **are**.

We _____ going to the park on Sunday.

What time _____ we going to leave?

Write a sentence using the word **are**.

sight words review

Name

Use the words in the word bank below to fill in the blanks for the sentences.

what	so	there
she	with	are

Guess _____ is in the big blue box.

I think she will get _____ before us.

What kind of shoes is _____ wearing?

The dogs _____ barking at the mailman.

I brought my favorite toy _____ me.

Let's hurry _____ we can get there soon.

sight word: **let**

Name

Trace the words and then write them on your own in the space below.

let   let   let   let

Color the word.

let

Complete the sentences by filling in the blanks with the word **let**.

We should _____ her play with us.

Don't _____ go of the kite string.

Write a sentence using the word **let**.

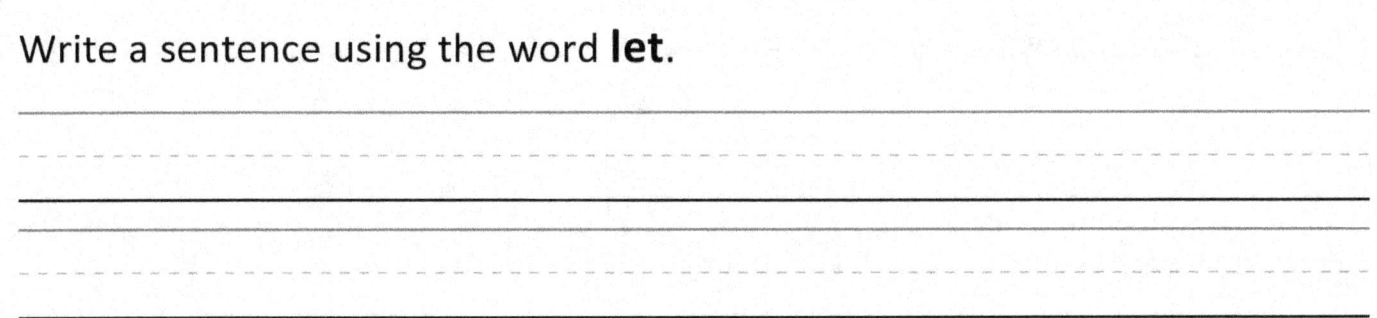

sight word: get

Name

Trace the words and then write them on your own in the space below.

get   get   get   get

Color the word.

get

Complete the sentences by filling in the blanks with the word **get**.

Where can I _____ a hat like that?

Can you _____ my cat out of the tree?

Write a sentence using the word **get**.

sight word: **our**

Name

Trace the words and then write them on your own in the space below.

our   our   our   our

Color the word.

our

Complete the sentences by filling in the blanks with the word **our**.

There are seven people on _____ team.

That is _____ house on the corner.

Write a sentence using the word **our**.

sight word: new

Name

Trace the words and then write them on your own in the space below.

new   new   new   new

Color the word.

new

Complete the sentences by filling in the blanks with the word **new**.

My sister gave me a _____ book.

I like using my _____ set of markers.

Write a sentence using the word **new**.

sight word: **soon**

Name

Trace the words and then write them on your own in the space below.

soon   soon   soon

Color the word.

soon

Complete the sentences by filling in the blanks with the word **soon**.

The movie will be starting _____.

We'll leave as _____ as we can.

Write a sentence using the word **soon**.

sight word: under

Name

Trace the words and then write them on your own in the space below.

under　　　under　　　under

Color the word.

under

Complete the sentences by filling in the blanks with the word **under**.

My shoes are _____ the chair.

I like to sit _____ the big oak tree.

Write a sentence using the word **under**.

sight words review

Name

Use the words in the word bank below to fill in the blanks for the sentences.

| under | our | soon |
| get | new | let |

A _____ student joined our class today.

He _____ us play with his new puppy.

The guests should arrive very _____.

The little kitten ran _____ the bed.

We should _____ a hat for the snowman.

Mr. Japson is _____ science teacher.

sight word: **who**

Name

Trace the words and then write them on your own in the space below.

who   who   who   who

Color the word.

who

Complete the sentences by filling in the blanks with the word **who**.

Do you know _____ drew this picture?

I wonder _____ left this toy on the table.

Write a sentence using the word **who**.

sight word: **four**

Name

Trace the words and then write them on your own in the space below.

four   four   four

Color the word.

four

Complete the sentences by filling in the blanks with the word **four**.

Jimmy has _____ yellow marbles.

The ball game starts at _____ o'clock.

Write a sentence using the word **four**.

sight word: as

Name

Trace the words and then write them on your own in the space below.

as   as   as   as

Color the word.

as

Complete the sentences by filling in the blanks with the word **as**.

Your hat is the same color _____ mine.

She waved to us _____ she ran by.

Write a sentence using the word **as**.

sight word: **white**

Name

Trace the words and then write them on your own in the space below.

white   white   white

Color the word.

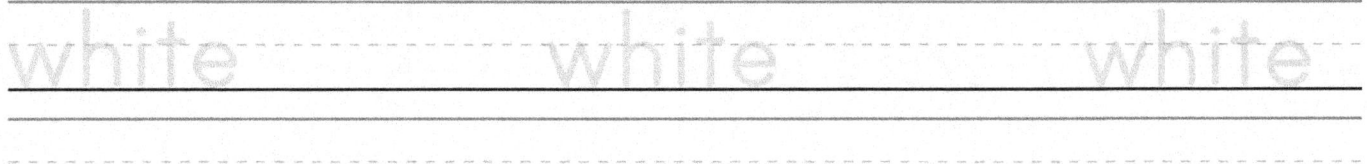

Complete the sentences by filling in the blanks with the word **white**.

The clouds look _____ and fluffy.

He is wearing a _____ shirt.

Write a sentence using the word **white**.

sight word: his

Name

Trace the words and then write them on your own in the space below.

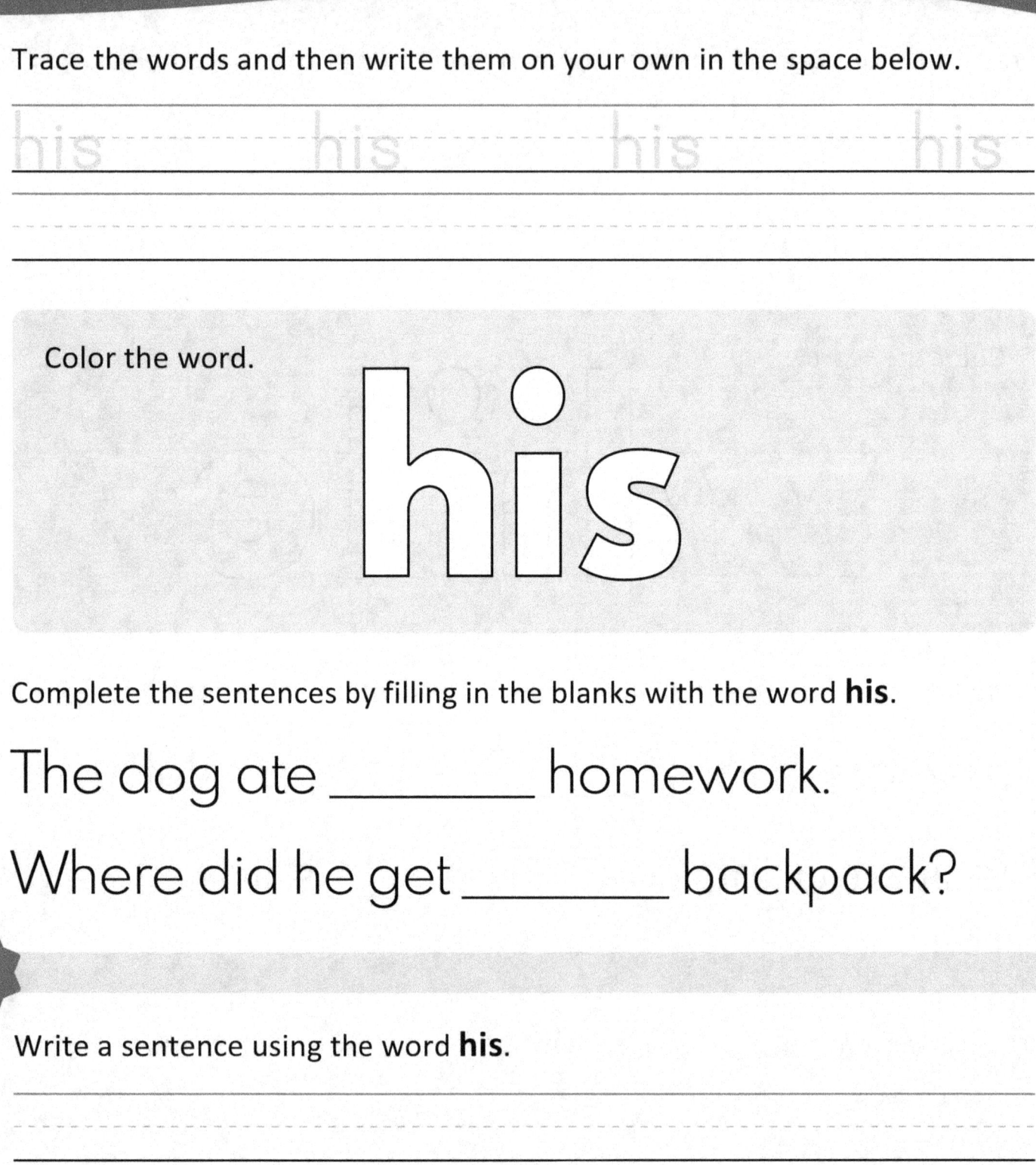

Color the word.

Complete the sentences by filling in the blanks with the word **his**.

The dog ate _____ homework.

Where did he get _____ backpack?

Write a sentence using the word **his**.

sight word: again

Name

Trace the words and then write them on your own in the space below.

again   again   again

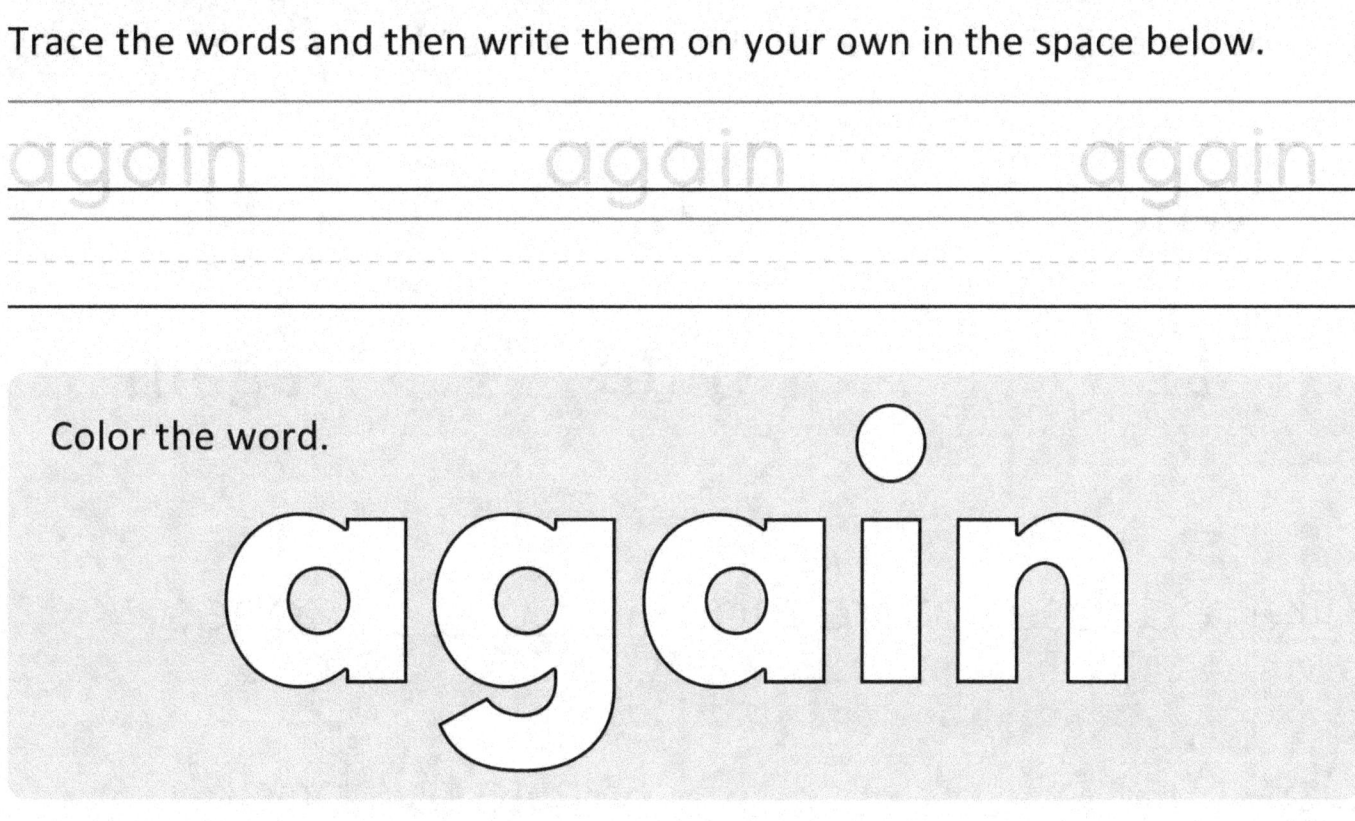

Color the word.

Complete the sentences by filling in the blanks with the word **again**.

We will see you _____ tomorrow.

Would you like to try that _____ ?

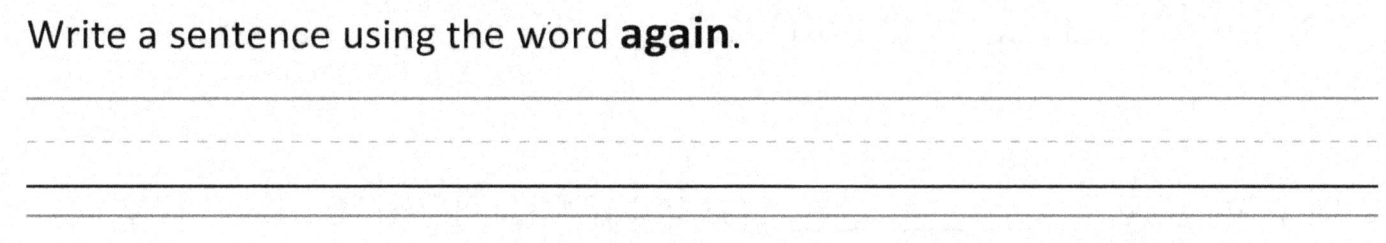

Write a sentence using the word **again**.

sight words review

Name

Use the words in the word bank below to fill in the blanks for the sentences.

| who | four | his |
| as | white | again |

I like red roses more than _____ ones.

Do you know _____ wrote this book?

Can we come back _____ tomorrow?

I will be back in _____ minutes.

Her birthday is the same _____ mine.

Bill forgot _____ backpack in the library.

sight word: **think**

Name

Trace the words and then write them on your own in the space below.

think   think   think

Color the word.

think

Complete the sentences by filling in the blanks with the word **think**.

I _____ she will like her gift.

Do you _____ it will rain today?

Write a sentence using the word **think**.

sight word: **over**

Name

Trace the words and then write them on your own in the space below.

over over over

Color the word.

over

Complete the sentences by filling in the blanks with the word **over**.

I saw geese fly _____ the pond.

The movie will be _____ soon.

Write a sentence using the word **over**.

sight word: **ask**

Name

Trace the words and then write them on your own in the space below.

ask   ask   ask   ask

Color the word.

ask

Complete the sentences by filling in the blanks with the word **ask**.

Joe raised his hand to _____ a question.

Did you _____ her to visit on Saturday?

Write a sentence using the word **ask**.

sight word: when

Name

Trace the words and then write them on your own in the space below.

when   when   when

Color the word.

when

Complete the sentences by filling in the blanks with the word **when**.

I like to swim _____ it's hot outside.

Let me know _____ you are ready.

Write a sentence using the word **when**.

sight word: fly

Name

Trace the words and then write them on your own in the space below.

fly　　　fly　　　fly　　　fly

Color the word.

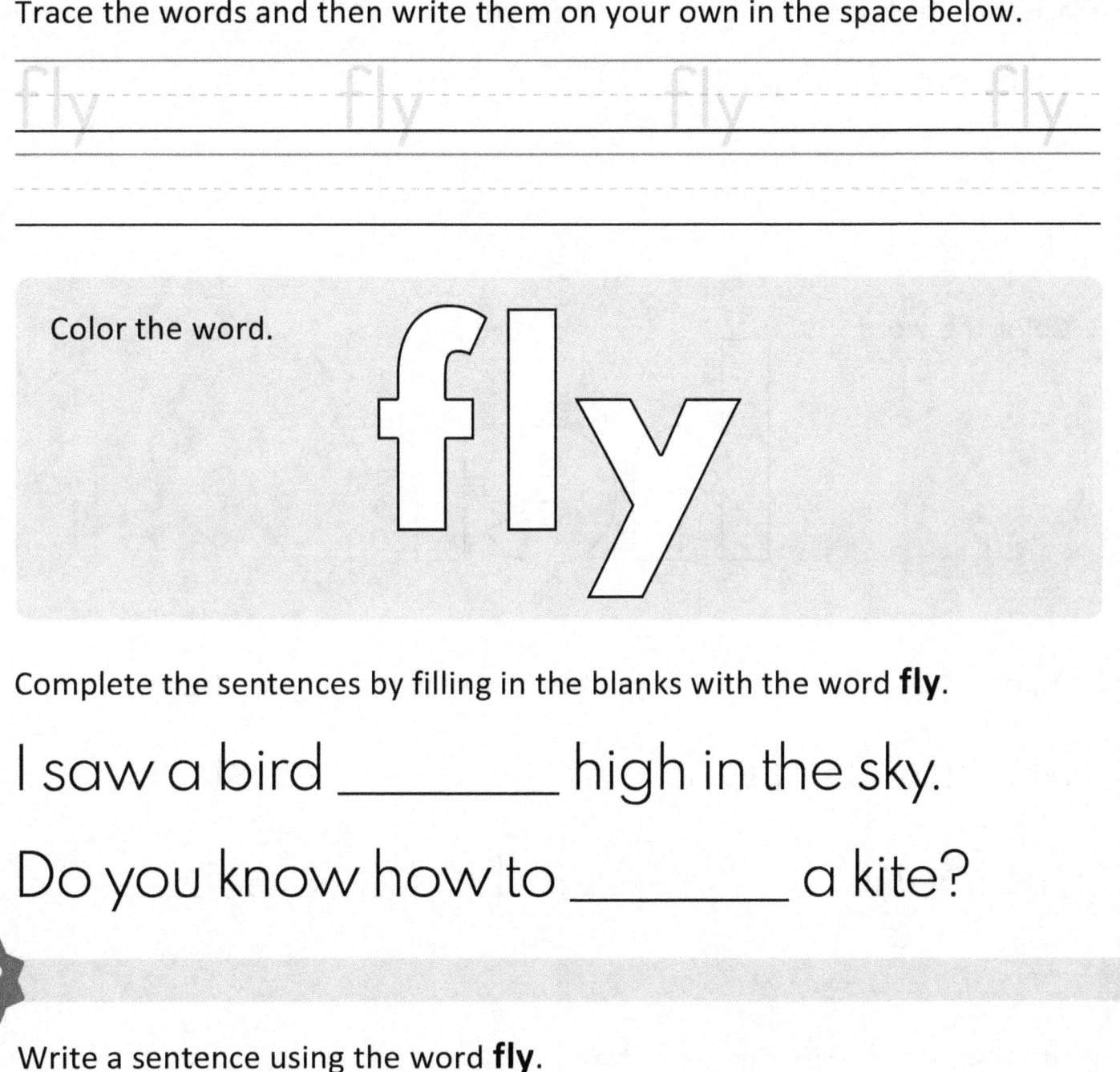

Complete the sentences by filling in the blanks with the word **fly**.

I saw a bird _____ high in the sky.

Do you know how to _____ a kite?

Write a sentence using the word **fly**.

sight word: her

Name

Trace the words and then write them on your own in the space below.

her   her   her   her

Color the word.

her

Complete the sentences by filling in the blanks with the word **her**.

The bird laid eggs in _____ nest.

She found _____ doll in the closet.

Write a sentence using the word **her**.

sight words review

Name

Use the words in the word bank below to fill in the blanks for the sentences.

| think | ask | her |
| over | fly | when |

I would like to _____ another question.

Sally ate _____ lunch in the backyard.

I want to be a pilot _____ I grow up.

The seagull flew _____ our heads.

Do you _____ our team will win the game?

The bird will _____ away if you go near it.

sight word: once

Name

Trace the words and then write them on your own in the space below.

once   once   once

Color the word.

once

Complete the sentences by filling in the blanks with the word **once**.

Steve goes bowling _____ in a while.

We like to visit them _____ a month.

Write a sentence using the word **once**.

sight word: by

Name

Trace the words and then write them on your own in the space below.

by   by   by   by

Color the word.

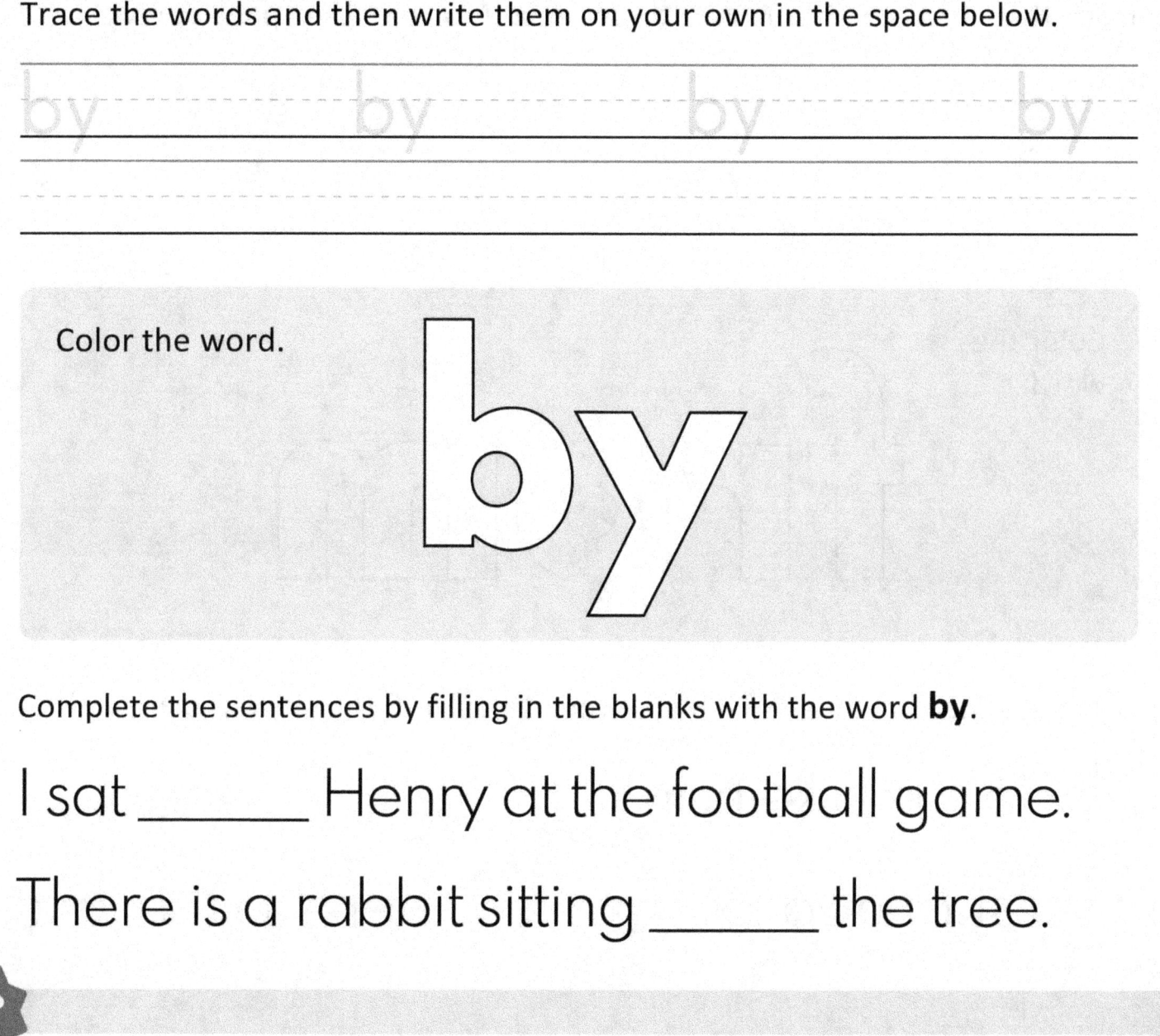

Complete the sentences by filling in the blanks with the word **by**.

I sat _____ Henry at the football game.

There is a rabbit sitting _____ the tree.

Write a sentence using the word **by**.

www.claymaze.com

sight word: **from**

Name

Trace the words and then write them on your own in the space below.

from　　　　from　　　　from

Color the word.

from

Complete the sentences by filling in the blanks with the word **from**.

I rode my bike home _____ school.

It's a short walk _____ here to the lake.

Write a sentence using the word **from**.

sight word: any

Name

Trace the words and then write them on your own in the space below.

any　　　any　　　any　　　any

Color the word.

any

Complete the sentences by filling in the blanks with the word **any**.

I don't see _____ clouds in the sky.

Is there _____ ice cream in the freezer?

Write a sentence using the word **any**.

sight word: just

Name

Trace the words and then write them on your own in the space below.

just   just   just

Color the word.   just

Complete the sentences by filling in the blanks with the word **just**.

We got there _____ in time.

She looks _____ like her twin sister.

Write a sentence using the word **just**.

sight word: **take**

Name

Trace the words and then write them on your own in the space below.

take   take   take

Color the word.

take

Complete the sentences by filling in the blanks with the word take.

The bus will _____ us home today.

Can we _____ a five minute break?

Write a sentence using the word take.

sight words review

Name

Use the words in the word bank below to fill in the blanks for the sentences.

from	any	once
by	take	just

The puppy is sleeping _____ the window.

You can choose _____ color you like.

I _____ heard that loud sound again.

She stood far away _____ the bee hive.

We usually ride our bikes _____ a week.

My aunt will _____ us to the beach today.

sight word: an

Name

Trace the words and then write them on your own in the space below.

an   an   an   an

Color the word.

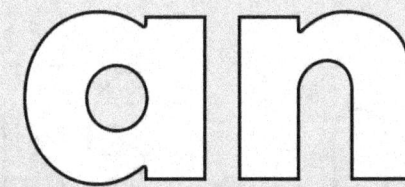

Complete the sentences by filling in the blanks with the word **an**.

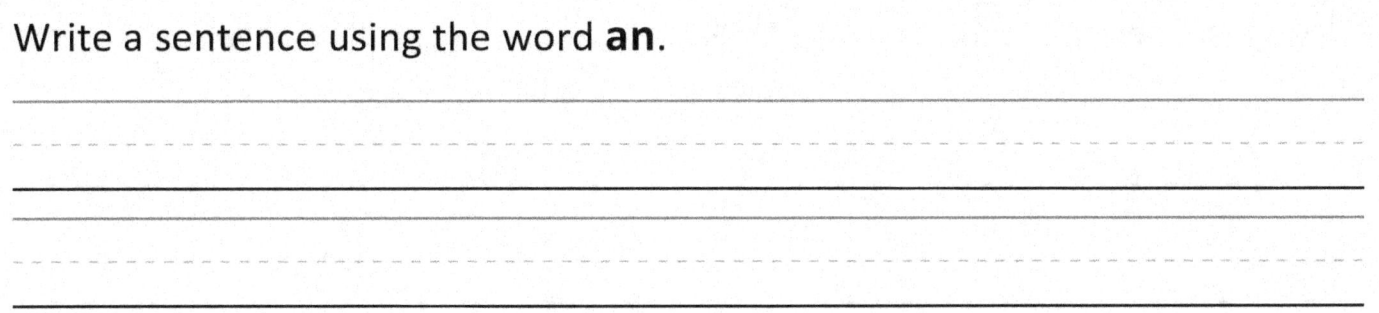

Write a sentence using the word **an**.

sight word: then

Name

Trace the words and then write them on your own in the space below.

then   *then*   *then*

Color the word.

then

Complete the sentences by filling in the blanks with the word then.

We played and _____ ate lunch.

She read a book _____ went to bed.

Write a sentence using the word then.

sight word: **put**

Name

Trace the words and then write them on your own in the space below.

put   put   put   put

Color the word.

put

Complete the sentences by filling in the blanks with the word **put**.

Will you _____ the fruit on the table?

Jerry _____ ice cream on his cake.

Write a sentence using the word **put**.

sight word: **stop**

Name

Trace the words and then write them on your own in the space below.

stop	stop	stop

Color the word.

stop

Complete the sentences by filling in the blanks with the word **stop**.

Can we _____ and get a snack?

It should _____ snowing by tonight.

Write a sentence using the word **stop**.

sight word: **thank**

Name

Trace the words and then write them on your own in the space below.

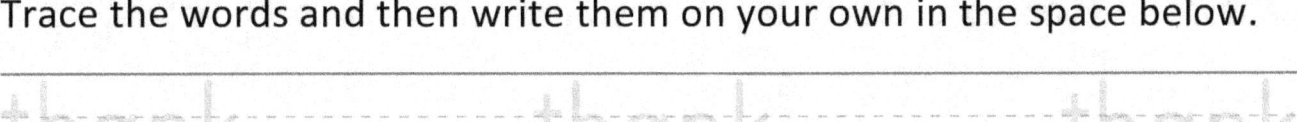

Color the word.

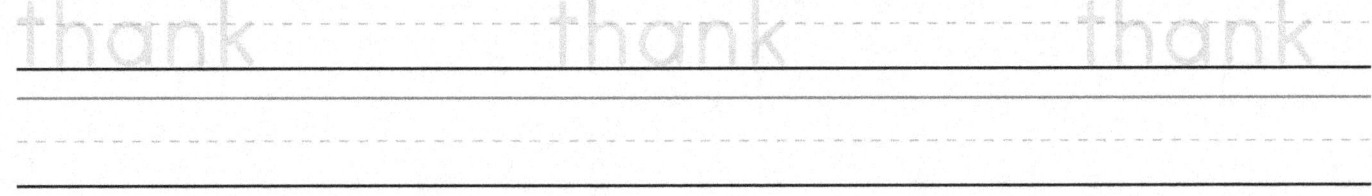

Complete the sentences by filling in the blanks with the word **thank**.

Let's _____ Daniel for his help.

We should _____ Jill for the cookies.

Write a sentence using the word **thank**.

www.claymaze.com

sight word: open

Name

Trace the words and then write them on your own in the space below.

open   open   open

Color the word.

open

Complete the sentences by filling in the blanks with the word **open**.

Will you _____ this jar for me?

Turn the knob to _____ the door.

Write a sentence using the word **open**.

sight words review

Name

Use the words in the word bank below to fill in the blanks for the sentences.

| put | then | open |
| thank | an | stop |

The baker _____ the cookies into a jar.

Would you like _____ apple or a pear?

Remember to _____ Andy for the gift.

Please _____ the door when she knocks.

We ate our dinner and _____ had dessert.

I hope the rain will _____ soon.

sight word: had

Name

Trace the words and then write them on your own in the space below.

had had had had

Color the word.

had

Complete the sentences by filling in the blanks with the word **had**.

The black cat _____ white spots.

She _____ grapes in her fruit basket.

Write a sentence using the word **had**.

sight word: were

Name

Trace the words and then write them on your own in the space below.

were   were   were

Color the word.

were

Complete the sentences by filling in the blanks with the word **were**.

They _____ all waiting for us outside.

There _____ two squirrels in the yard.

Write a sentence using the word **were**.

sight word: after

Name

Trace the words and then write them on your own in the space below.

after		after		after

Color the word.

after

Complete the sentences by filling in the blanks with the word **after**.

The number four is _____ three.

Let's play a game _____ dinner.

Write a sentence using the word **after**.

sight word: **round**

Name

Trace the words and then write them on your own in the space below.

round　　　round　　　round

Color the word.

round

Complete the sentences by filling in the blanks with the word **round**.

We all sat at the _____ table.

I see a _____ window on the wall.

Write a sentence using the word **round**.

sight word: could

Name

Trace the words and then write them on your own in the space below.

could   could   could

Color the word.

could

Complete the sentences by filling in the blanks with the word could.

We _____ leave early tomorrow.

She ran as fast as she _____.

Write a sentence using the word could.

sight word: give

Name

Trace the words and then write them on your own in the space below.

give　　　　　　　give　　　　　　　give

Color the word.

give

Complete the sentences by filling in the blanks with the word **give**.

I will _____ him a toy for his birthday.

Please _____ this book to your sister.

Write a sentence using the word **give**.

sight words review

Name

Use the words in the word bank below to fill in the blanks for the sentences.

| round | had | give |
| after | were | could |

We went to the playground _____ school.

She _____ a bouncy castle at her party.

There was a little _____ table in the room.

Please _____ this note to James.

We _____ at the parade yesterday.

I didn't know he _____ speak French.

sight word: **has**

Name

Trace the words and then write them on your own in the space below.

has   has   has   has

Color the word.

has

Complete the sentences by filling in the blanks with the word **has**.

That spider _____ eight eyes!

Melissa _____ three green iguanas.

Write a sentence using the word **has**.

sight word: **them**

Name

Trace the words and then write them on your own in the space below.

them　　　　　them　　　　　them

Color the word.

them

Complete the sentences by filling in the blanks with the word **them**.

I gave the cookies to all of _____.

Please ask _____ to come inside.

Write a sentence using the word **them**.

sight word: **of**

Name

Trace the words and then write them on your own in the space below.

of   of   of   of

Color the word.

of

Complete the sentences by filling in the blanks with the word **of**.

Millie was afraid _____ the chicken.

Car tires are made _____ rubber.

Write a sentence using the word **of**.

145   www.claymaze.com

sight word: live

Name

Trace the words and then write them on your own in the space below.

live   live   live

Color the word.

live

Complete the sentences by filling in the blanks with the word **live**.

Polar bears _____ near the North Pole.

Penguins _____ near the South Pole.

Write a sentence using the word **live**.

sight word: every

Name

Trace the words and then write them on your own in the space below.

every   every   every

Color the word.

every

Complete the sentences by filling in the blanks with the word **every**.

We wake up early _____ morning.

I visit my aunt _____ Sunday.

Write a sentence using the word **every**.

sight word: **how**

Name

Trace the words and then write them on your own in the space below.

how how how how

Color the word.

how

Complete the sentences by filling in the blanks with the word **how**.

Will you teach me _____ to cook?

Do you know _____ to swim?

Write a sentence using the word **how**.

sight words review

Name

Use the words in the word bank below to fill in the blanks for the sentences.

| every | how | live |
| has | of | them |

It was time for all of _____ to leave.

Jane eats vegetables _____ day.

I am learning _____ to make pizza.

Quincy _____ a fig tree in his yard.

She stood in front _____ the warm fire.

We _____ in the blue house on the corner.

sight word: **him**

Name

Trace the words and then write them on your own in the space below.

him   him   him   him

Color the word.

him

Complete the sentences by filling in the blanks with the word **him**.

I went with _____ to the pet shop.

Please throw the ball to _____.

Write a sentence using the word **him**.

sight word: **know**

Name

Trace the words and then write them on your own in the space below.

know   know   know

Color the word.

know

Complete the sentences by filling in the blanks with the word **know**.

Do you _____ when the party starts?

I _____ how to throw a frisbee.

Write a sentence using the word **know**.

sight word: walk

Name

Trace the words and then write them on your own in the space below.

walk walk walk

Color the word.

walk

Complete the sentences by filling in the blanks with the word **walk**.

Can we _____ a little faster?

I can _____ to my house from here.

Write a sentence using the word **walk**.

sight word: old

Name

Trace the words and then write them on your own in the space below.

Color the word.

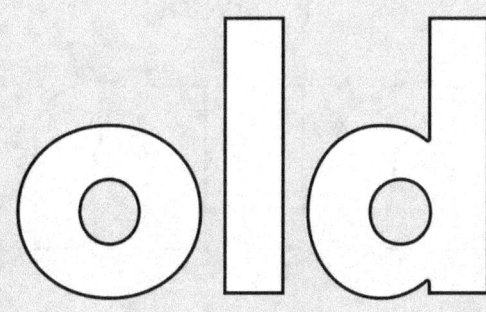

Complete the sentences by filling in the blanks with the word **old**.

My big brother is eight years _____.

How _____ is this dinosaur fossil?

Write a sentence using the word **old**.

sight word: going

Name

Trace the words and then write them on your own in the space below.

going   *going*   *going*

Color the word.

going

Complete the sentences by filling in the blanks with the word **going**.

When are you _____ to the game?

We are _____ to Aunt Jackie's house.

Write a sentence using the word **going**.

sight word: **some**

Name

Trace the words and then write them on your own in the space below.

some　　　　　some　　　　　some

Color the word.

some

Complete the sentences by filling in the blanks with the word **some**.

You have _____ milk on your chin.

Would you like _____ popcorn?

Write a sentence using the word **some**.

sight words review

Name

Use the words in the word bank below to fill in the blanks for the sentences.

| old | walk | know |
| going | him | some |

We are _____ to a restaurant tonight.

Do you _____ what type of cat that is?

She gave the yellow box to _____.

Would you like to _____ with us to school?

My _____ shirt has lots of holes.

I need _____ batteries for my flashlight.

SECTION 2

NOUNS

72 Word Focus Pages
12 Word Bank Review Pages

ClayMaze.com

SECTION 2 WORD LIST

nest	school	egg
rain	fish	box
children	boat	eye
ground	floor	water
ring	game	birthday
rabbit	father	girl
house	ball	song
car	garden	paper
snow	shoe	bird
baby	wood	hand
hill	party	squirrel
picture	thing	farmer
wind	street	bed
coat	watch	window
flower	toy	cake
head	apple	duck
dog	chicken	mother
sister	fire	tree
feet	bread	milk
table	door	chair
money	stick	doll
boy	farm	corn
cow	brother	horse
bell	cat	grass

noun: **nest**

Name

Trace the words and then write them on your own in the space below.

nest   nest   nest

Complete the sentences by filling in the blanks with the word **nest**.

I see a bird's _____ in the tree.

The alligator's _____ is near the water.

Draw a picture of a **nest** and write a sentence about it on the lines below.

noun: **rain**

Name

Trace the words and then write them on your own in the space below.

rain　　　　　rain　　　　　rain

Complete the sentences by filling in the blanks with the word **rain**.

We should wait until the _____ stops.

I hear _____ falling on the roof.

Draw a picture of **rain** and write a sentence about it on the lines below.

noun: **children**

Name

Trace the words and then write them on your own in the space below.

children   children   children

Complete the sentences by filling in the blanks with the word **children**.

There are _____ playing outside.

The _____ made paper airplanes.

Draw a picture of **children** and write a sentence about it on the lines below.

noun: **ground**

Name

Trace the words and then write them on your own in the space below.

ground　　*ground*　　*ground*

Complete the sentences by filling in the blanks with the word **ground**.

We planted seeds in the _____.

The _____ is covered with snow.

Draw a picture of the **ground** and write a sentence about it on the lines below.

noun: **ring**

Name

Trace the words and then write them on your own in the space below.

ring　　　　　ring　　　　　ring

Complete the sentences by filling in the blanks with the word **ring**.

She wore a gold _____ on her finger.

I put my _____ into the jewelry box.

Draw a picture of a **ring** and write a sentence about it on the lines below.

noun: **rabbit**

Name

Trace the words and then write them on your own in the space below.

rabbit   rabbit   rabbit

Complete the sentences by filling in the blanks with the word **rabbit**.

My friend has a pet _____.

The little _____ has floppy ears.

Draw a picture of a **rabbit** and write a sentence about it on the lines below.

www.claymaze.com

nouns review

Name

Use the words in the word bank below to fill in the blanks for the sentences.

| rabbit | rain | children |
| nest | ground | ring |

Jeremy bounced the ball on the _____.

The _____ painted in art class today.

There are three eggs in the _____.

I am wearing a _____ on my index finger.

The _____ made puddles on the ground.

The furry _____ hopped across the field.

noun: house

Name

Trace the words and then write them on your own in the space below.

house   house   house

Complete the sentences by filling in the blanks with the word house.

We live in a red brick _____.

Scott's _____ is on the corner.

Draw a picture of a house and write a sentence about it on the lines below.

noun: **car**

Name

Trace the words and then write them on your own in the space below.

car   car   car   car

Complete the sentences by filling in the blanks with the word **car**.

My uncle drives a silver _____.

The _____ stopped at the traffic light.

Draw a picture of a **car** and write a sentence about it on the lines below.

noun: **snow**

Name

Trace the words and then write them on your own in the space below.

snow   snow   snow

Complete the sentences by filling in the blanks with the word **snow**.

The _____ fell slowly to the ground.

His hair was covered with _____.

Draw a picture of **snow** and write a sentence about it on the lines below.

noun: **baby**

Name

Trace the words and then write them on your own in the space below.

baby   baby   baby

Complete the sentences by filling in the blanks with the word **baby**.

The little _____ is asleep in her crib.

She gave the _____ a bottle of milk.

Draw a picture of a **baby** and write a sentence about it on the lines below.

noun: **hill**

Name

Trace the words and then write them on your own in the space below.

hill　　　hill　　　hill　　　hill

Complete the sentences by filling in the blanks with the word **hill**.

We all sat on the grassy _____.

We followed the trail up the _____.

Draw a picture of a **hill** and write a sentence about it on the lines below.

noun: **picture**

Name

Trace the words and then write them on your own in the space below.

picture   picture   picture

Complete the sentences by filling in the blanks with the word **picture**.

He painted a _____ of the beach.

A _____ of our family is on the wall.

Draw a picture of a **picture** and write a sentence about it on the lines below.

www.claymaze.com

nouns review

Name

Use the words in the word bank below to fill in the sentences.

| picture | hill | baby |
| snow | house | car |

We rode a sled down the snowy _____.

They live in a brick _____ on Pine Street.

She rocked the _____ to help her sleep.

I took a _____ of a pretty butterfly.

The warm sun melted the _____.

My brother rode in the _____ with us.

noun: **wind**

Name

Trace the words and then write them on your own in the space below.

wind   wind   wind

Complete the sentences by filling in the blanks with the word **wind**.

I feel the cold _____ on my face.

The _____ blew out the candle.

Draw a picture about **wind** and write a sentence about it on the lines below.

noun: **coat**

Name

Trace the words and then write them on your own in the space below.

coat   coat   coat

Complete the sentences by filling in the blanks with the word **coat**.

Remember to wear your _____ today.

His _____ kept him warm in the snow.

Draw a picture of a **coat** and write a sentence about it on the lines below.

noun: **flower**

Name

Trace the words and then write them on your own in the space below.

flower　　　flower　　　flower

Complete the sentences by filling in the blanks with the word **flower**.

Please put the _____ in a vase.

The _____ grew from a seed.

Draw a picture of a **flower** and write a sentence about it on the lines below.

noun: head

Name

Trace the words and then write them on your own in the space below.

head   head   head

Complete the sentences by filling in the blanks with the word **head**.

He rested his _____ on the soft pillow.

A ladybug landed on my _____.

Draw a picture of a **head** and write a sentence about it on the lines below.

noun: **dog**

Name

Trace the words and then write them on your own in the space below.

dog   dog   dog   dog

Complete the sentences by filling in the blanks with the word **dog**.

Mr. Flatican is walking his _____.

My _____ likes to play fetch with sticks.

Draw a picture of a **dog** and write a sentence about it on the lines below.

www.claymaze.com

noun: **sister**

Name

Trace the words and then write them on your own in the space below.

sister   *sister*   *sister*

Complete the sentences by filling in the blanks with the word **sister**.

My _____ is younger than me.

I like to play cards with my _____.

Draw a picture of a **sister** and write a sentence about it on the lines below.

nouns review

Name

Use the words in the word bank below to fill in the blanks for the sentences.

| flower | coat | sister |
| head | dog | wind |

My _____ drove me to school today.

There is a pretty red _____ in the garden.

The _____ is barking at a squirrel.

She held an umbrella over her _____.

Which direction is the _____ blowing?

I wear my warm _____ in cold weather.

noun: **feet**

Name

Trace the words and then write them on your own in the space below.

feet   feet   feet

Complete the sentences by filling in the blanks with the word **feet**.

Socks will keep my _____ warm.

I have two hands and two _____.

Draw a picture of **feet** and write a sentence about it on the lines below.

noun: **table**

Name

Trace the words and then write them on your own in the space below.

table   table   table

Complete the sentences by filling in the blanks with the word **table**.

We all sat down to eat at the _____.

Our dinner _____ is made of glass.

Draw a picture of a **table** and write a sentence about it on the lines below.

noun: money

Name

Trace the words and then write them on your own in the space below.

money   money   money

Complete the sentences by filling in the blanks with the word **money**.

I brought _____ to buy a new ball.

Did you bring _____ for the movie?

Draw a picture of **money** and write a sentence about it on the lines below.

noun: **boy**

Name

Trace the words and then write them on your own in the space below.

boy   boy   boy   boy

Complete the sentences by filling in the blanks with the word **boy**.

The little _____ is rolling a toy car.

The _____ is wearing a baseball cap.

Draw a picture of a **boy** and write a sentence about it on the lines below.

noun: COW

Name

Trace the words and then write them on your own in the space below.

cow　　　cow　　　cow　　　cow

Complete the sentences by filling in the blanks with the word **cow**.

There is a brown _____ in the field.

Have you ever milked a _____ ?

Draw a picture of a **COW** and write a sentence about it on the lines below.

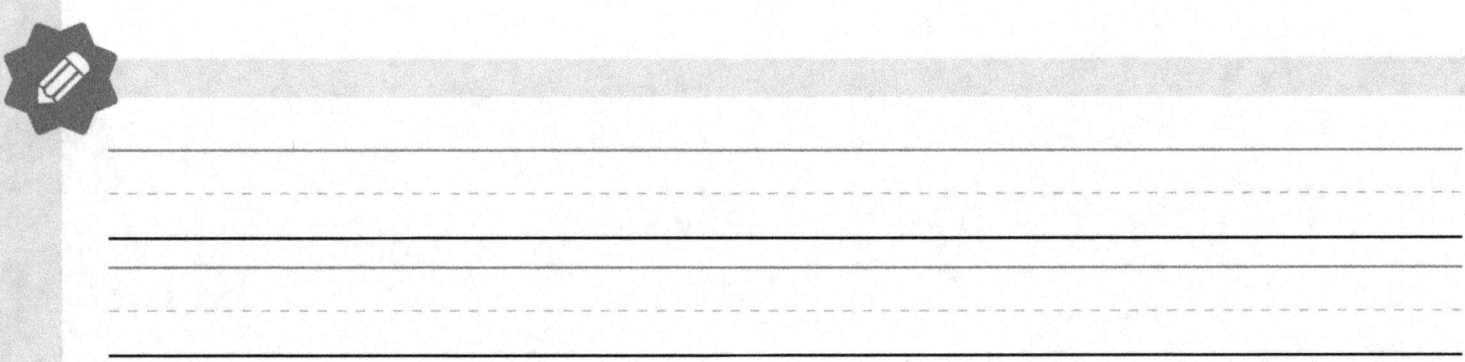

noun: **bell**

Name

Trace the words and then write them on your own in the space below.

bell　　　　　bell　　　　　bell

Complete the sentences by filling in the blanks with the word **bell**.

Do you want to ring the _____?

The _____ will ring at eleven o'clock.

Draw a picture of a **bell** and write a sentence about it on the lines below.

nouns review

Name _____

Use the words in the word bank below to fill in the blanks for the sentences.

| money | feet | table |
| cow | boy | bell |

I sat at the _____ to do my homework.

She took her shoes off of her _____.

We all went outside after the _____ rang.

The _____ stays in the barn when it rains.

I have enough _____ to buy a milkshake.

The _____ is bouncing a bright red ball.

noun: **school**

Name

Trace the words and then write them on your own in the space below.

school   school   school

Complete the sentences by filling in the blanks with the word **school**.

The bus drops us off at _____.

Emily walks to _____ every day.

Draw a picture of a **school** and write a sentence about it on the lines below.

noun: **fish**

Name

Trace the words and then write them on your own in the space below.

fish   fish   fish

Complete the sentences by filling in the blanks with the word **fish**.

Did you catch any _____ today?

I saw lots of _____ in the aquarium.

Draw a picture of a **fish** and write a sentence about it on the lines below.

noun: **boat**

Name

Trace the words and then write them on your own in the space below.

boat   boat   boat

Complete the sentences by filling in the blanks with the word **boat**.

We rowed a _____ across the pond.

My brother likes to fish from his _____.

Draw a picture of a **boat** and write a sentence about it on the lines below.

noun: **floor**

Name

Trace the words and then write them on your own in the space below.

floor　　　　floor　　　　floor

Complete the sentences by filling in the blanks with the word **floor**.

There is a soft rug on the _____.

We all sat on the _____ in a circle.

Draw a picture of a **floor** and write a sentence about it on the lines below.

noun: game

Name

Trace the words and then write them on your own in the space below.

game　　　game　　　game

Complete the sentences by filling in the blanks with the word **game**.

What is your favorite video _____ ?

The football _____ starts at noon.

Draw a picture of a **game** and write a sentence about it on the lines below.

noun: **father**

Name

Trace the words and then write them on your own in the space below.

father   father   father

Complete the sentences by filling in the blanks with the word **father**.

I played basketball with my _____.

Erin's _____ drove us to the fair.

Draw a picture of a **father** and write a sentence about it on the lines below.

nouns review

Name

Use the words in the word bank below to fill in the blanks for the sentences.

| father | boat | school |
| fish | floor | game |

Would you like to play a _____ with us?

I learned how to paint in _____ today.

We all crossed the lake in a _____.

I see _____ swimming in the lake.

My _____ and I went fishing on Saturday.

The tile _____ is cold in the winter.

noun: **ball**

Name

Trace the words and then write them on your own in the space below.

ball　　　　　ball　　　　　ball

Complete the sentences by filling in the blanks with the word **ball**.

Mia hit the _____ over the net.

The _____ bounced down the stairs.

Draw a picture of a **ball** and write a sentence about it on the lines below.

noun: garden

Name

Trace the words and then write them on your own in the space below.

garden   garden   garden

Complete the sentences by filling in the blanks with the word **garden**.

I saw a rabbit in the _____.

We planted flowers in the _____.

Draw a picture of a **garden** and write a sentence about it on the lines below.

noun: shoe

Name

Trace the words and then write them on your own in the space below.

shoe   shoe   shoe

Complete the sentences by filling in the blanks with the word **shoe**.

What size _____ do you wear?

There is a hole in my left _____.

Draw a picture of a **shoe** and write a sentence about it on the lines below.

www.claymaze.com

noun: **wood**

Name

Trace the words and then write them on your own in the space below.

wood   wood   wood

Complete the sentences by filling in the blanks with the word **wood**.

The coffee table is made of _____.

Dad chopped _____ for the fireplace.

Draw a picture of **wood** and write a sentence about it on the lines below.

noun: **party**

Name

Trace the words and then write them on your own in the space below.

party   party   party

Complete the sentences by filling in the blanks with the word **party**.

His birthday _____ is on Saturday.

What time does the _____ start?

Draw a picture of a **party** and write a sentence about it on the lines below.

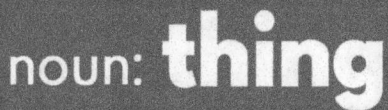

Name

Trace the words and then write them on your own in the space below.

thing thing thing

Complete the sentences by filling in the blanks with the word **thing**.

I don't know what that _____ is.

Everyone wanted the same _____.

Draw a picture of a **thing** and write a sentence about it on the lines below.

www.claymaze.com

nouns review

Name

Use the words in the word bank below to fill in the blanks for the sentences.

| garden | ball | wood |
| party | shoe | thing |

My right _____ just fell off of my foot.

We are growing tomatoes in our _____.

I kicked the _____ across the soccer field.

Her birthday _____ starts at two o'clock.

I just wanted to say one more _____.

This picnic table is made of _____.

noun: **street**

Name

Trace the words and then write them on your own in the space below.

street　　　　street　　　　street

Complete the sentences by filling in the blanks with the word **street**.

Which _____ do you live on?

My friend lives across the _____.

Draw a picture of a **street** and write a sentence about it on the lines below.

noun: **watch**

Name

Trace the words and then write them on your own in the space below.

watch watch watch

Complete the sentences by filling in the blanks with the word **watch**.

My brother has a digital _____.

Cindy wears a _____ on her wrist.

Draw a picture of a **watch** and write a sentence about it on the lines below.

noun: **toy**

Name

Trace the words and then write them on your own in the space below.

toy   toy   toy   toy

Complete the sentences by filling in the blanks with the word **toy**.

He gave his sister a new _____.

My favorite _____ is made of wood.

Draw a picture of a **toy** and write a sentence about it on the lines below.

noun: **apple**

Name

Trace the words and then write them on your own in the space below.

apple   apple   apple

Complete the sentences by filling in the blanks with the word **apple**.

Jim took a bite out of the _____.

She gave an _____ to the teacher.

Draw a picture of an **apple** and write a sentence about it on the lines below.

noun: **chicken**

Name

Trace the words and then write them on your own in the space below.

chicken   chicken   chicken

Complete the sentences by filling in the blanks with the word **chicken**.

The _____ just laid an egg!

A _____ ran into the barn.

Draw a picture of a **chicken** and write a sentence about it on the lines below.

noun: **fire**

Name

Trace the words and then write them on your own in the space below.

fire   fire   fire

Complete the sentences by filling in the blanks with the word **fire**.

The hot _____ burned brightly.

We sat by the _____ to stay warm.

Draw a picture of **fire** and write a sentence about it on the lines below.

nouns review

Name _____

Use the words in the word bank below to fill in the blanks for the sentences.

| chicken | toy | street |
| apple | watch | fire |

The _____ ate some cracked corn.

Would you like an orange or an _____ ?

They used water to put out the _____.

The time on my _____ is eight o'clock.

Look both ways before crossing the _____.

The children are playing with a _____.

noun: bread

Name

Trace the words and then write them on your own in the space below.

bread   bread   bread

Complete the sentences by filling in the blanks with the word **bread**.

He baked the _____ in the oven.

I learned how to make _____ .

Draw a picture of **bread** and write a sentence about it on the lines below.

noun: **door**

Name

Trace the words and then write them on your own in the space below.

door   door   door

Complete the sentences by filling in the blanks with the word **door**.

Please keep the _____ closed.

The _____ to the classroom was open.

Draw a picture of a **door** and write a sentence about it on the lines below.

noun: **stick**

Name

Trace the words and then write them on your own in the space below.

stick   stick   stick

Complete the sentences by filling in the blanks with the word **stick**.

A _____ fell from the old tree.

Her dog ran to fetch the _____.

Draw a picture of a **stick** and write a sentence about it on the lines below.

noun: farm

Name

Trace the words and then write them on your own in the space below.

farm　　　　farm　　　　farm

Complete the sentences by filling in the blanks with the word **farm**.

I rode a tractor on the _____.

Their _____ has a big red barn.

Draw a picture of a **farm** and write a sentence about it on the lines below.

noun: **brother**

Name

Trace the words and then write them on your own in the space below.

brother   brother   brother

Complete the sentences by filling in the blanks with the word **brother**.

I talked to my _____ on the phone.

My _____ likes to play football.

Draw a picture of a **brother** and write a sentence about it on the lines below.

noun: **cat**

Name

Trace the words and then write them on your own in the space below.

cat   cat   cat   cat

Complete the sentences by filling in the blanks with the word **cat**.

I have an orange tabby _____.

His _____ chased a squirrel up the tree.

Draw a picture of a **cat** and write a sentence about it on the lines below.

nouns review

Name

Use the words in the word bank below to fill in the sentences.

| brother | door | farm |
| cat | stick | bread |

Please lock the _____ when you leave.

We grow vegetables on our _____.

I bought a loaf of _____ from the grocery.

Our pet _____ likes to play with yarn.

My _____ and sister are older than me.

She broke a _____ off of the tree.

noun: egg

Name

Trace the words and then write them on your own in the space below.

egg   egg   egg   egg

Complete the sentences by filling in the blanks with the word **egg**.

I ate a fried _____ for breakfast.

The chicken laid an _____ in the barn.

Draw a picture of an **egg** and write a sentence about it on the lines below.

noun: **box**

Name

Trace the words and then write them on your own in the space below.

box   box   box   box

Complete the sentences by filling in the blanks with the word **box**.

Let's open the _____ to see what's inside.

Chad gave me a _____ of chocolates.

Draw a picture of a **box** and write a sentence about it on the lines below.

noun: **eye**

Name

Trace the words and then write them on your own in the space below.

eye   eye   eye   eye

Complete the sentences by filling in the blanks with the word **eye**.

That dog's right _____ is blue.

Some sand just blew into my _____.

Draw a picture of an **eye** and write a sentence about it on the lines below.

noun: **water**

Name

Trace the words and then write them on your own in the space below.

water   water   water

Complete the sentences by filling in the blanks with the word **water**.

Marie drank a glass of cold _____.

Let's boil some _____ to make tea.

Draw a picture of **water** and write a sentence about it on the lines below.

noun: **birthday**

Name

Trace the words and then write them on your own in the space below.

birthday   birthday   birthday

Complete the sentences by filling in the blanks with the word **birthday**.

My _____ is in the summer.

We made a card for her _____.

Draw a picture about a **birthday** and write a sentence about it on the lines below.

noun: **girl**

Name

Trace the words and then write them on your own in the space below.

girl　　　　　girl　　　　　girl

Complete the sentences by filling in the blanks with the word **girl**.

The _____ is wearing a pink dress.

Debbie is a _____ from my school.

Draw a picture of a **girl** and write a sentence about it on the lines below.

nouns review

Name

Use the words in the word bank below to fill in the blanks for the sentences.

| birthday | egg | water |
| eye | girl | box |

The sprinkler sprayed us with _____.

The pirate covered his _____ with a patch.

A baby bird just hatched from its _____.

The _____ was open, so I peeked inside.

We baked a cake for Roger's _____.

The little _____ is holding her pet rabbit.

noun: **song**

Name

Trace the words and then write them on your own in the space below.

song   song   song

Complete the sentences by filling in the blanks with the word **song**.

The band played my favorite _____.

Let's all sing a _____ together.

Draw a picture about a **song** and write a sentence about it on the lines below.

noun: **paper**

Name

Trace the words and then write them on your own in the space below.

paper   paper   paper

Complete the sentences by filling in the blanks with the word **paper**.

Trees are used to make _____.

He folded _____ into animal shapes.

Draw a picture of **paper** and write a sentence about it on the lines below.

noun: **bird**

Name

Trace the words and then write them on your own in the space below.

bird   bird   bird

Complete the sentences by filling in the blanks with the word **bird**.

That _____ has beautiful red feathers.

I see a _____ sitting in its nest.

Draw a picture of a **bird** and write a sentence about it on the lines below.

noun: hand

Name

Trace the words and then write them on your own in the space below.

hand　　　　hand　　　　hand

Complete the sentences by filling in the blanks with the word **hand**.

She held a book in her right _____.

I raised my _____ to ask a question.

Draw a picture of a **hand** and write a sentence about it on the lines below.

noun: **squirrel**

Name

Trace the words and then write them on your own in the space below.

squirrel   squirrel   squirrel

Complete the sentences by filling in the blanks with the word **squirrel**.

That _____ is eating a nut.

A _____ just ran up the oak tree.

Draw a picture of a **squirrel** and write a sentence about it on the lines below.

noun: farmer

Name

Trace the words and then write them on your own in the space below.

farmer   farmer   farmer

Complete the sentences by filling in the blanks with the word **farmer**.

The _____ is planting seeds.

I saw a _____ driving a tractor.

Draw a picture of a **farmer** and write a sentence about it on the lines below.

nouns review

Name

Use the words in the word bank below to fill in the blanks for the sentences.

| farmer | song | squirrel |
| hand | paper | bird |

We cut shapes out of colored _____.

The _____ burried a nut in the ground.

My favorite _____ is playing on the radio.

A yellow _____ flew over the roof.

What are you holding in your _____?

The _____ grew lots of vegetables.

noun: **bed**

Name

Trace the words and then write them on your own in the space below.

bed   bed   bed   bed

Complete the sentences by filling in the blanks with the word **bed**.

My cat ran under the _____ to get his toy.

Both kids were jumping on the _____.

Draw a picture of a **bed** and write a sentence about it on the lines below.

noun: window

Name

Trace the words and then write them on your own in the space below.

window   window   window

Complete the sentences by filling in the blanks with the word **window**.

My cat likes to sit by the _____.

Please keep the _____ closed.

Draw a picture of a **window** and write a sentence about it on the lines below.

noun: **cake**

Name

Trace the words and then write them on your own in the space below.

cake   cake   cake

Complete the sentences by filling in the blanks with the word **cake**.

What is your favorite type of _____ ?

My mother baked a _____ for us.

Draw a picture of a **cake** and write a sentence about it on the lines below.

noun: duck

Name

Trace the words and then write them on your own in the space below.

duck   duck   duck

Complete the sentences by filling in the blanks with the word **duck**.

That _____ just quacked at us!

The _____ is floating on the water.

Draw a picture of a **duck** and write a sentence about it on the lines below.

noun: **mother**

Name

Trace the words and then write them on your own in the space below.

mother   mother   mother

Complete the sentences by filling in the blanks with the word **mother**.

My _____ gave me a necklace.

I went to a movie with my _____.

Draw a picture of a **mother** and write a sentence about it on the lines below.

noun: **tree**

Name

Trace the words and then write them on your own in the space below.

tree   tree   tree

Complete the sentences by filling in the blanks with the word **tree**.

I saw a cone fall from the pine _____.

There is an old oak _____ in the yard.

Draw a picture of a **tree** and write a sentence about it on the lines below.

nouns review

Name _____

Use the words in the word bank below to fill in the sentences.

| mother | duck | window |
| tree | cake | bed |

Would you like a slice of birthday _____?

We saw a _____ swim across the pond.

The little boy is asleep in his _____.

I closed the _____ when it began to rain.

Her _____ baked cookies for the class.

We had a picnic under the shade _____.

noun: **milk**

Name

Trace the words and then write them on your own in the space below.

milk   milk   milk

Complete the sentences by filling in the blanks with the word **milk**.

I drank a glass of _____ for breakfast.

Charlie likes to drink chocolate _____.

Draw a picture of **milk** and write a sentence about it on the lines below.

noun: chair

Name

Trace the words and then write them on your own in the space below.

chair   chair   chair

Complete the sentences by filling in the blanks with the word **chair**.

She sat on the wooden _____.

My dad's office _____ has wheels.

Draw a picture of a **chair** and write a sentence about it on the lines below.

noun: doll

Name

Trace the words and then write them on your own in the space below.

doll   doll   doll

Complete the sentences by filling in the blanks with the word **doll**.

The little girl is holding a _____.

The _____ is wearing a green dress.

Draw a picture of a **doll** and write a sentence about it on the lines below.

noun: **corn**

Name

Trace the words and then write them on your own in the space below.

corn   corn   corn

Complete the sentences by filling in the blanks with the word **corn**.

We saw fields of _____ at the farm.

I ate some _____ with my dinner.

Draw a picture of **corn** and write a sentence about it on the lines below.

noun: **horse**

Name

Trace the words and then write them on your own in the space below.

horse   horse   horse

Complete the sentences by filling in the blanks with the word **horse**.

Do you know how to ride a _____ ?

I fed an apple to the _____ .

Draw a picture of a **horse** and write a sentence about it on the lines below.

noun: **grass**

Name

Trace the words and then write them on your own in the space below.

grass grass grass

Complete the sentences by filling in the blanks with the word **grass**.

The _____ was wet from the rain.

Children are playing on the _____.

Draw a picture of **grass** and write a sentence about it on the lines below.

nouns review

Use the words in the word bank below to fill in the blanks for the sentences.

| grass | corn | horse |
| doll | chair | milk |

I have a beanbag _____ in my room.

The _____ has hair made of yarn.

I saw a _____ jump over the fence.

She poured _____ in her cereal.

We played frisbee on the _____.

Do you like to eat _____ on the cob?

SECTION

SOLUTIONS

Solutions to Review Pages

ClayMaze.com

PAGE: 9

make
down
can
big
not
the

PAGE: 16

little
and
one
help
where
go

PAGE: 23

find
we
come
is
three
my

PAGE: 30

up
for
a
said
look
blue

PAGE: 37

to
funny
jump
red
here
in

PAGE: 44

play
I
yellow
it
see
away

PAGE: 51

have
went
me
two
will
run

PAGE: 58

did
eat
pretty
you
ride
at

PAGE: 65

he
out
black
like
good
be

PAGE: 72

all
well
was
brown
no
they

PAGE: 79

too
am
came
into
yes
this

PAGE: 86

that
saw
now
but
say
want

PAGE: 93

ate
do
ran
on
please
must

PAGE: 100

what
there
she
are
with
so

PAGE: 107

new
let
soon
under
get
our

PAGE: 114

white
who
again
four
as
his

PAGE: 121

ask
her
when
over
think
fly

PAGE: 128

by
any
just
from
once
take

PAGE: 135

put
an
thank
open
then
stop

PAGE: 142

after
had
round
give
were
could

PAGE: 149

them
every
how
has
of
live

PAGE: 156

going
know
him
walk
old
some

PAGE: 165

ground
children
nest
ring
rain
rabbit

PAGE: 172

hill
house
baby
picture
snow
car

PAGE: 179

sister
flower
dog
head
wind
coat

PAGE: 186

table
feet
bell
cow
money
boy

PAGE: 193

game
school
boat
fish
father
floor

PAGE: 200

shoe
garden
ball
party
thing
wood

PAGE: 207

chicken
apple
fire
watch
street
toy

PAGE: 214

door
farm
bread
cat
brother
stick

PAGE: 221

water
eye
egg
box
birthday
girl

PAGE: 228

paper
squirrel
song
bird
hand
farmer

PAGE: 235

cake
duck
bed
window
mother
tree

PAGE: 242

chair
doll
horse
milk
grass
corn

www.ingramcontent.com/pod-product-compliance
Lightning Source LLC
Chambersburg PA
CBHW081741100526
44592CB00015B/2258